The *TREND*advisor Guide to Breakthrough Profits

Founded in 1807, John Wiley & Sons is the oldest independent publishing company in the United States. With offices in North America, Europe, Australia, and Asia, Wiley is globally committed to developing and marketing print and electronic products and services for our customers' professional and personal knowledge and understanding.

The Wiley Trading series features books by traders who have survived the market's ever changing temperament and have prospered—some by reinventing systems, others by getting back to basics. Whether a novice trader, professional, or somewhere in-between, these books will provide the advice and strategies needed to prosper today and well into the future.

For a list of available titles, please visit our Web site at www.Wiley Finance.com.

The *TREND*advisor Guide to Breakthrough Profits

A Proven System for Building Wealth in the Financial Markets

CHUCK DUKAS with T. Parker Gallagher

WILEY

John Wiley & Sons, Inc.

Published by John Wiley & Sons, Inc., Hoboken, New Jersey.
Published simultaneously in Canada.

For general information on our other products and services or for technical support, please contact our Customer Care Department within the United States at (800) 762-2974, outside the United States at (317) 572-3993 or fax (317) 572-4002.

Wiley also publishes its books in a variety of electronic formats. Some content that appears in print may not be available in electronic books. For more information about Wiley products, visit our web site at www.wiley.com.

Library of Congress Cataloging-in-Publication Data:

Dukas, Chuck, 1949–
    The TRENDadvisor guide to breakthrough profits : a proven system
for building wealth in the financial markets / Chuck Dukas.
      p. cm. — (Wiley trading series)
    Includes index.
    ISBN-13: 978-0-471-75147-2 (cloth)
    ISBN-10: 0-471-75147-2 (cloth)
    1. Stocks. 2. Investment analysis. I. Title. II. Title: TRENDadvisor guide to
breakthrough profits. III. Series.
    HG4661.D85   2006
    332.63'22—dc22

                                    2005031903

Printed in the United States of America.

10 9 8 7 6 5 4 3 2 1

Contents

Foreword

The history of technical analysis in the United States dates back to the late 1800s; it was Charles H. Dow who expressed his thoughts about the activity of the stock market and the sentiment of investors. His belief in the primary, secondary, and minor movements of price set the stage for what we all know and accept as technical analysis. In fact, he went further by describing the emotions of fear and greed evidenced in the activity of investors and traders alike; his writings on sentiment were the forerunners of what university professors now call behavioral finance. He and many other writers have contributed to our understanding of the basic forces that dominate the marketplace today: supply and demand.

The latest adaptation of these basic principles is found in Chuck Dukas' book *The TRENDadvisor Guide to Breakthrough Profits: A Proven System for Building Wealth in the Stock Market*. Early on, this author talks about the need for methodology and the understanding of who is doing either the trading or the investing. Knowing the difference between the two, he feels, will help in creating the discipline and the knowledge we must all have to best analyze trends and use them in trading and investing. Like Dow, Dukas states that there is a clear distinction between price movements; and, with the advantage of modern-day tools, he has created a combination of technical indicators that form his TRENDadvisor Diamond.

The buy side and sell side of the Diamond highlight the technical traits found when demand dominates the action of buyers and conversely when the characteristics of supply overwhelm and the sellers take control of the action. By establishing specific criteria that define each phase, the book breaks trends into separate components. Each phase describes a distinct price movement. This book explains how the indicators are created and distinguishes how they behave in each separate phase, aiding the reader in learning how to interpret them. Each chapter describes how the forces of buyers and sellers play out in the charts, making it easier for the reader to understand the dynamics of supply and demand. The author writes about the need to include analysis in a methodology and plan. The detailed analysis of the sell side covers an important topic that many people overlook of how to take profits, and also offers a useful explanation of short selling.

Thorough, detailed, and useful technical analysis like what is offered in this book continues a trend of wider acceptance of technical analysis. The release date of this book follows shortly after the most important event to ever happen to technical analysis since Charles Dow's first articles of price activity appeared in the *Wall Street Journal*. It came in the form of the Securities and Exchange Commission (SEC)'s recognition of technical analysis. In March 2005, the SEC amended Rule #344. It now reads: "There are officially two analysts in Wall Street; a fundamental analyst follows companies and a technical analyst follows stocks." This watershed event has placed technical analysis on a par with fundamental analysis. Never in its history has this subject been so recognized and accepted by the establishment. The organization that gets the credit for this historic achievement is the Market Technicians Association (MTA). Many hardworking members of the MTA helped raise the standard for this deserving subject.

And it is authors like Chuck Dukas who continue to raise the bar for all of us when he writes that technical indicators will act differently during the six stages of his Diamond. He wants his readers to understand that we should all approach the market with a trading plan and the discipline to carry out that plan. Enjoy Chuck's book—I certainly did.

—Ralph Acampora

Acknowledgments

I dedicate this book to those individuals who have contributed emotionally, physically, spiritually, and professionally to this undertaking. With their support the dream became a reality.

First, to my wife Judy for your willingness *always* to support my efforts and to assist in bringing this vision into focus without distraction.

To my children, Jessica and Mark, for their patience and sacrifice allowing me to complete this project.

To my in-laws, Domenic and Grace DeMunda for personal direction and family values I have learned from them over the years.

To T. Parker Gallagher, my colleague who assisted me with taking my intellectual property and putting it into words.

Introduction

This is a book about teaching you how to approach making money in the markets. How can you make money by trading or investing in the financial markets? Our answer is by having a methodology, consistently applying it, controlling risk to preserve capital, and taking profits. What we will do for you in this book is help you to develop a methodology so you can determine whether a stock, mutual fund, commodity, or any other financial instrument is something you want to own—either as an investment or as a trade. What we are going to teach you is how to analyze any financial instrument to determine whether it is a candidate for your investment or trading dollars. There is a variety of ways to make money in the markets. You can be an investor or a trader. In our world, investors tend to have longer time horizons; traders tend to be shorter term oriented. The common objective of both is making money in the markets.

For all market participants, there are two important decisions to make—when to get in and when to get out, or when to enter and when to exit. Where the exit is relative to the entry dictates the outcome of the trade or investment—profit or loss. What you use to determine your entry and your exit is your methodology. This book is about how to create your own methodology for trading or investing in financial instruments.

Your methodology for entries and exits is not the only important decision you must make. You also have to decide how many positions or trades you will carry, at a maximum, and how much capital you will devote to any single position. You will need to decide how much risk you will take in any single position by defining where your stop loss will be placed. Your stop is the amount of capital that will be forever gone from your account when it is triggered. It is one of two possible exits from your trade or investment. The other is your profit target—the area where you will be starting to liquidate your winning investment or trade. Most traders have no set methodology for harvesting profits. We encourage a different approach of having a defined methodology that helps set a target and harvesting part of your profits when it is achieved.

You will make more decisions when you select what you will be investing or trading. Stocks? Futures? Indexes (including exchange traded funds)? Commodities? Foreign exchange? Mutual funds? What timeframe will you be using—are your trades or investments going to be held for a few days or a week? Months? Years? What are your objectives? How much capital are you going to devote to reaching them?

The answers to these various questions are all part of a trading plan—an organized approach to how you will be doing your trading or investing. Trading or investing is like any business or economically motivated endeavor in that success is much more likely to come from a defined methodology, consistently applied, with good risk control—in short, a well organized plan—than by chance or random selections. In Chapter 10 we will guide you into creating a trading or investing plan of your own. As you read this book, please keep in mind that you are learning what you need to know to create a trading plan for yourself.

An example of a simple methodology that many mutual fund owners, who have subscribed to the "buy and hold" approach, use is to own funds in their retirement accounts. They buy mutual funds, often periodically with every paycheck, and hold them until retirement. As the market goes up and down, they sit through the gyrations. They sell, or exit, on retirement day or when they need the money during retirement. There is a methodology in this—a defined strategy for buying, holding (under the theory that time will make you money), and selling—only when the money is needed in retirement.

The managers of those mutual funds, the folks who invest that money, also have some kind of methodology. Frequently it is to analyze a number of companies across industries, and find ones that their spreadsheet model says will grow in a manner that their calculations say they can now buy at a discount based on their predictions of future value. They then wait for the company to grow and the stock price to go up to reflect the value of that growth. They sell when the stock price is higher than the discounted future value calculation says it should be.

However, this is only theory. The reality is that the Investment Company Institute calculates the average turnover in mutual funds is 100 percent per year. This means that, on average, fund managers are buying and selling every stock in their portfolio once a year, which hardly qualifies as long term investing. This tells us that there is a tremendous amount of trading going on in mutual funds. This, combined with the fact that most mutual funds underperform the indexes, suggests that those investing methodologies do not translate successfully into profitable trading strategies.

The point is this: Everyone needs a methodology. Few have one that they consistently apply. If you are actively managing financial assets of any kind—stocks, mutual funds, or commodities—your methodology should include the criteria for how and why you are buying what you are buying, and the criteria for how and why you are selling what you are selling.

Our approach has a simple underlying rationale: buy and own only stocks or instruments that meet the criteria of an uptrend. For those who have the sophistication and for whom it is appropriate, sell or sell short stocks or financial instruments that meet the criteria of a downtrend. The definitions of uptrend and downtrend come from how the prices of these instruments are behaving. This puts us in the world of technical analysis. There is no fundamental analysis in our methodology—no discounted cash flow models, earnings estimates, industry predictions, or present value calculations.

When you enter your position, your outcome is going to be a function of what the other market participants are doing. If you trade with them, you will profit. If you trade against them, you probably will not. Therefore, you should have an understanding of who the players are, their methodology for decision making, and how they are paid (which is a proxy for motivation). You will find your job of making money in the markets easier if you understand the dynamics of how these players make their decisions and use that information in your own decision-making.

Why do stocks and other financial instruments go up and down? The price at which a stock/instrument trades at any moment in time is the balance of supply and demand for that stock/instrument at that time. Different participants have different determinations of what something is worth at any point in time. If something is rallying, going up, there may be a large-volume trader who decides it is time to take a profit and sell. This will cause the price to stop going up or to go down. Likewise, if something is going down, a large investor may have a model that says, at this price it is worth buying. This will cause the price to stop declining or go up.

Who are these other market participants you are trading with or against? They are the sum of all market participants, but we can categorize them into three distinct groups. The first is mutual funds and other professional investors (money managers). Next come hedge funds. Some hedge funds are investor oriented, but there are many that are trading oriented. The third group includes the trading desks of the major Wall Street brokerage firms and other professional traders (which can include trading oriented hedge funds).

Mutual funds are run by a fund manager or managers. One becomes a mutual fund portfolio manager by having been a good analyst. The path to becoming an analyst is: first, graduate from an excellent college, then work at an investment bank or mutual fund for two or three years, building spreadsheet models of companies' income and expenses and predicting how the income and expenses will play out under various circumstances. Then go to a top business school (two more years), build more spreadsheet models, after which get a job as an analyst at a mutual fund or brokerage firm. If the analyst is good and makes good recommendations to the portfolio managers, after three to five years she may be offered a portfolio to run. Mutual fund managers are graded by beating the benchmark, by how much they outperform the index their fund is compared to. Note that this does not mean they have to make money—in a down market, all they have to do is be down less than the market to earn their bonus—and bonuses are the greater part of their pay. They beat their benchmark frequently by looking at all the industries and companies in the benchmark, deciding what is likely to underperform, and buying everything else. Or, they will load up on (overweight) what they think will outperform and underweight everything else. Like professional money managers, they have to wait to get their profits—usually for quarters and years, because it takes time for the companies they are buying to experience the growth they are forecasting. Their decision inputs include what the analysts are discovering and advising (both buy side and sell side analysts), and what the companies tell them. It is estimated that the total investment amount of mutual funds is about one trillion dollars.

Hedge funds come in all shapes and sizes. Like mutual funds, they are pools of money put up by their investors. However, they differ from mutual funds in several aspects. First, hedge fund managers are paid a percentage of the profits the fund earns. This gives them a huge incentive—they are paid on actual profits earned, not by beating some benchmark. This is called absolute performance as opposed to relative performance. Second, not only can they buy stocks, they can also short them; see the next paragraph for a description of short selling. Because these managers can short, they can make money in markets, stocks, or instruments that are going down. Finally, hedge funds can use leverage—they can borrow money to increase the amount they invest. This magnifies the fund's returns (and also its losses!). Hedge funds are incredibly lucrative. Pay scales there are vastly higher than at mutual funds. This means that the best portfolio managers and analysts frequently leave mutual funds to set up their own hedge funds. For the fundamentally oriented funds, the manager's decision inputs include what the analysts are discovering and advising (both buy side and sell side analysts), and what the companies tell them. Because they are paid on what they make, they will frequently trade in and out of positions, taking advantage of market moves to generate profits. Many use sophisticated algorithms—mathematical models—to make their buy and sell decisions. It is estimated that hedge funds' total investment is about one trillion dollars. Note that this makes them about the same size as the mutual fund industry—they just have different tactics and objectives.

Short selling is a tactic employed by sophisticated traders to profit from things that are going down, not up, in price. To conceptualize this, let's use a fictional story. Pretend that your analysis suggests that a company's stock is about to decline from its current price of $50 and you would like to profit from that decline. You call your friendly broker and tell him you would like to short 100 shares of the stock. He goes into his book of clients and finds a fellow who owns a bunch of this stock. He calls the fellow up and asks if the fellow would "lend" some of the stock and be paid some interest for lending it. The fellow says, "Let me see if I understand you. You would like to borrow some of my shares of stock. I will still own them. And you will pay me interest for lending them to you. Is that correct?" "Yes," replies the broker. "Okay." So the fellow lends the 100 shares to you. You take the borrowed 100 shares, sell them in the market for $50 and collect the proceeds ($5,000 less commissions, which you keep in your brokerage account). The stock falls to $40. The fellow calls the broker: "Remember the shares I lent you? I want them back now because I want to sell the stock." The broker calls you. "The lender wants his shares back." "No problem," you say. "Take some of the money in my account and buy 100 shares of stock at the current price of $40. Then return the 100 shares to the lender." Your broker does this. You had sold the borrowed 100 shares at $50, collecting $5,000. You bought back those sold shares at $40, for $4,000. The stock has gone down 10 points and you have made $1,000.

Please note there are a number of substantial risks in shorting stocks, including, but not limited to, the company getting taken over and the stock price soaring. If the stock price goes up when you are short, you will have losses because you have to buy back the stock at a higher price than you sold it for.

Because of these risks, short selling is only for sophisticated traders. However, it is widely used by hedge funds, which are extremely sophisticated, and the big Wall Street trading desks. It is estimated that hedge funds control almost $1 trillion dollars, which is about the size of all mutual funds combined. Because of this, selling pressure in markets is not just from folks who own something selling it. Selling pressure in markets also includes short sellers. Short sellers are one of the significant reasons downtrends show pronounced selling.

Who do mutual fund players and hedge funds sell to and buy from? The trading desks of the largest Wall Street firms. These trading desks are very short term oriented; they will be in and out of positions in hours or days. Their inputs include sophisticated mathematical models that help determine the price to pay. Interestingly, we calculate that the total capital the largest Wall Street trading desks have to deploy in the market is about one trillion dollars. This means they are as well funded as the mutual funds and the hedge funds.

How do these three, equally well-capitalized players who each control about a trillion dollars, interact on any given day? The hedge funds who trade the indexes have sophisticated mathematical models that determine whether they should be buying or selling. The other professional traders (including the trading desks) react to these waves of buying and selling. Mutual fund managers are buying and selling based on updated information from the analysts and companies. In earnings seasons, those four times per year when companies report their quarterly earnings, the mutual fund managers will be quite active, updating their positions based on how the companies are performing. They sell out of, and buy into their positions, with the trading desks. Because they are longer-term investors (in theory), and they make their decisions based on the flow of information that impacts their spreadsheet models, they are not very sensitive to the price they pay or sell at. When it is time to buy, they buy; when time to sell, they sell. They buy and sell from the sophisticated traders who are only in those positions for a short period of time, and for whom price is everything—thus, they set the price in the short term. The mutual fund investors are less active at times outside of earnings season because there is less information on which to make decisions. This means the trading models have much more influence in how the market and stocks behave outside of earnings season.

Commodities have their own sets of players. If one thinks of agricultural commodities, there are producers (corn farmers), the users of those commodities (Kellogg's, who buys corn for cereals), and traders who are simply trying to make a profit. The longer-term price trends in commodities are a result of the underlying drivers of the supply and demand for that commodity. For example, a drought will kill off the corn crop, reducing supply. Prices rise—this is good for farmers who have corn, but bad for the consumers of corn.

To summarize, in the short term, the market is influenced by the professional traders; in the longer term, it is influenced by investors. Align your decision making and trade selection with the underlying dynamics of the demand and supply of the instruments you are trading. In short, trade with the trend! We will now explore how you can effectively analyze for trend.

CHAPTER 1

The Ins and Outs of Trends with a Toolkit for Analysis

Years ago *Fortune* magazine ran a powerful campaign about its media power under the slogan, "There is nothing more powerful than a trend." In reality, there is something even more powerful than a trend, and that is being able to perceive the beginnings and ends of trends. To be able to do that is to be able to take full advantage of knowing when to be in and when to be out. As Shakespeare said, "There is a tide in the affairs of men, which, taken at the flood, leads on to fortune."

Trading and investing is the art of deploying capital as prices change over time. When we analyze market behavior we are looking at two interactions: how price is changing (or not changing) over time; and whether or not the current price is behaving in a manner that indicates an action.

Our goal as investors and traders is to overcome fear and greed by trading what we *see*, not what we think or feel. Conceptually, trading and investing is putting capital at risk over time, and profits (or losses) are the outcome when we exit our trades. Trading is easiest when our capital produces profits quickly. Quick profits in short time frames are possible if we are trading in an instrument that is strongly trending. Then we should be continuously harvesting profits.

We define an uptrend as higher highs and higher lows over time. The faster prices rise in a shorter time frame indicates the strength of that uptrend, or shows how quickly higher highs can be achieved over time. Conversely, lower lows and lower highs are what characterize downtrends. The faster prices fall in shorter time frames allows us to calculate the strength of the downtrend. (A tool used for precise calculations, the 60 period high/low channel, will be described later.)

Our job as an investor or trader, therefore, is to recognize a trend and to identify when that trend is ending. If an uptrend is a series of highs, what does the end of that trend look like? Most traders would say it looks like a series of lows. However, more accurately, the end of an uptrend can just be an absence of further highs.

From either a trading or investing perspective, when our financial instrument breaks out into a series of new highs, we usually have our quickest, greatest profits in short time frames. Likewise, when we are short and it breaks down into lower lows, we frequently have our quickest, largest profits in short periods of time. We define a new series of highs as an emerging uptrend and a new series of lows as an emerging downtrend. Additionally, when there is an absence of new highs over time, that uptrend has potentially ended and likewise, on the down side, when there are no further new lows over time that downtrend has potentially ended.

60 PERIOD HIGH/LOW CHANNEL

We can track highs by using an indicator that draws the value of what the highest high has been for the last 60 periods. We then can see where the current price is relative to whatever the highest high has been for the last 60 periods. When price starts to exceed this line, the market is now producing the higher highs that define an uptrend. We use 60 periods because that is three months of trading data, one calendar quarter in the annual earnings cycle. (See Figure 1.1.)

If price has been going sideways for some time, there will be no new higher highs and the 60 period highest high indicator will go flat, indicating a potential end of trend.

We can also track lows by using an indicator that draws the value of what the lowest low has been for the last 60 periods. We then can see where the current price is relative to whatever the lowest low has been for the last 60 periods. When price starts to fall through this line, the market is now producing the lower lows that define a downtrend (see Figure 1.2).

If price has been going sideways for some time, there will be no new lower lows and the 60 period lowest low indicator will go flat, indicating a potential end of the downtrend.

We now have an indicator that tracks highs and an indicator that tracks lows. These help us to see the trend as it unfolds. We add to these two indicators a third: the 50 percent retracement indicator. This simple indicator shows the middle of the channel created by the 60 period high/low channel. It is calculated by summing the value of the high and low channels, then dividing by two. As you will see later, the 50 percent retracement line can be useful in making trading decisions in the trend (see Figure 1.3).

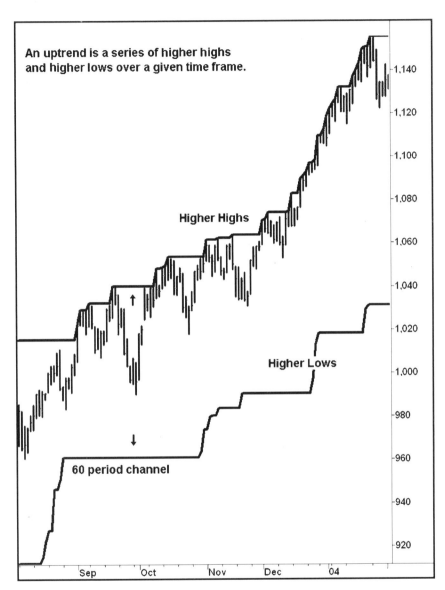

FIGURE 1.1 Uptrend with 60 Period High/Low Channel
Source: © TradeStation Technologies, Inc. 1991–2005

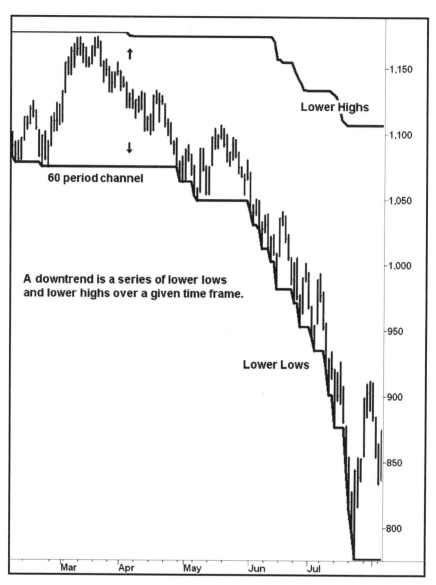

FIGURE 1.2 Downtrend with 60 Period High/Low Channel
Source: © TradeStation Technologies, Inc. 1991–2005

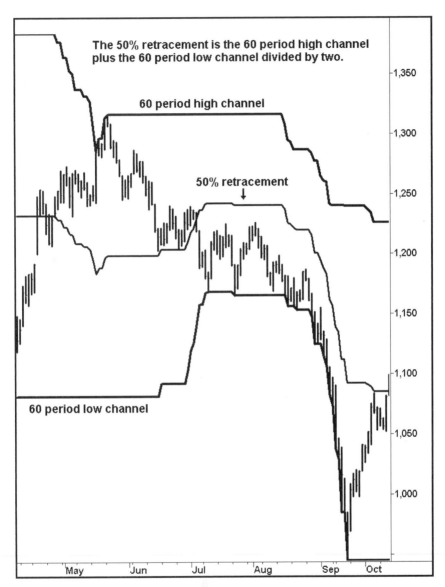

FIGURE 1.3 Fifty Percent Retracement of the 60 Period High/Low Channel
Source: © TradeStation Technologies, Inc. 1991–2005

"Bullish" is shorthand for upward price action. However, not all upward price action is indicative of further trend. In order to determine that upward price action is bullish, that price action needs to be viewed in the context of what has preceded the current price action. By comparing current price action to recent and longer term price action, we can classify current prices into specific phases, thus offering an objective definition of price phase. There are a number of ways to determine the context preceding the current price action. For the sake of simplicity, uniformity, and availability, we use moving averages.

Moving averages provide smoothing, which evens out the variability of short term price movement. They are also useful as comparative tools, where a shorter term moving average is compared to one of a longer length. This comparative feature means price can be rated to both recent as well as longer term averages, meaning current price can be rated in the context of recent as well as long term price. Most importantly, the slope (direction) of a moving average is an excellent tool for trend analysis.

Moving averages are calculated by simply summing a series of prices, then dividing by the number of prices in the series. A 3 period moving average with the numbers 24, 25, 26 sums to 75, which is then divided by number of observations, 3, to give an average value of 25. On a chart, the last price plot will be 26, and the moving average plot will be 25. If the next number in the series is 27, the new 3 period moving average will be the three observations of 25, 26, 27, summing to 78, which divided by 3 averages 26. The price plot is now 27 and the moving average plot is now 26. In this simple example, you can see that prices are closing above the moving average, and the moving average is increasing (from 25 to 26). This is upward and indicates positive slope.

If we have a series of prices, many of which are higher than a specific period of preceding prices, and we average all of the current time period prices, what would we find? We would find that this moving average, as time unfolds, has been increasing as prices went up.

Arithmetically, a series of higher highs and higher lows translates into a moving average that will slope upward, and as price action continues over time, this will result in the longer term moving average sloping upward. Using daily price data, we use the 50 period simple moving average, which is ten weeks of price action (or most of a quarterly earnings reporting cycle). This is sufficiently responsive to reflect the changing dynamics of price behavior without being unduly influenced by short term swings (see Figure 1.4).

If prices trend sideways for weeks (little change), you can see that the average of those prices will start to equalize. This will cause the moving average to flatten out, indicative of lack of trend in the price action.

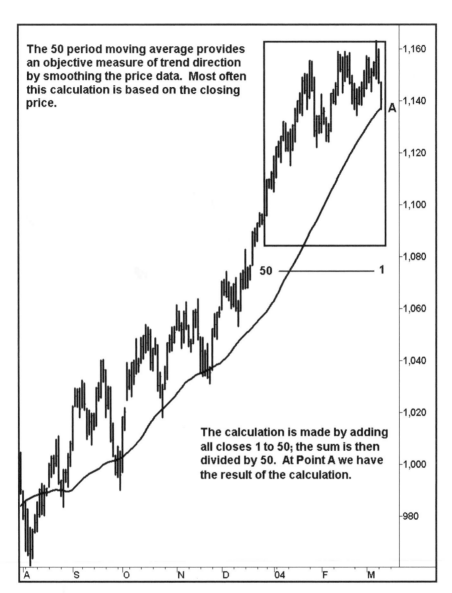

The 50 period moving average provides an objective measure of trend direction by smoothing the price data. Most often this calculation is based on the closing price.

50 ———————————— 1

The calculation is made by adding all closes 1 to 50; the sum is then divided by 50. At Point A we have the result of the calculation.

FIGURE 1.4 Calculating the 50 Period Moving Average
Source: © TradeStation Technologies, Inc. 1991–2005

A 50 period moving average is an excellent tool for seeing recent trend. We can supplement our analysis of trend by looking at a moving average that represents longer trend.

A moving average of 200 periods, which represents 40 weeks of trading data (just over three earnings quarters), captures the longer-term dynamic of changing price behavior. These two commonly used indicators are institutional "rudders," showing how the market is steered.

Why use a 200 period moving average in addition to a 50 period moving average? Our job as traders is to identify trends and effectively trade them because trading with trend provides us the quickest, biggest profit in the shortest period. Usually, trends do not end quickly nor do they end with a sharp, substantial reversal in price. Therefore, a longer moving average can better help us to see the longer trend of prices, which can enable us to be trading with that trend.

Additionally, the longer moving average takes into account the prime movers of markets and prices: institutions! Institutional infusion of cash from mutual funds, hedge funds, money management firms, and trading desks are the primary forces that drive the markets, and thus create the short, medium, and long term price and volume trends.

These national and global players work with millions upon millions of shares of equity; they are responsible for the lion's share of the two to four billion shares traded per day on the major U.S. markets. Our study of the Dow Jones Industrial Average 16-year cycle looked for discernible inflection points and patterns in the DJIA. One of our key observations was that the Dow's moves can be specifically analyzed using the 50 period and 200 period moving averages. These two commonly used indicators are institutional "rudders" and show distinct patterns over the past 71 years. If the 200 period moving average is up, generally it shows that institutions are buying the market. If the 200 period moving average is down, usually it shows that institutions are selling the market. Given those facts, why argue with a gorilla? Only if you want to lose! (See Figure 1.5.)

One of the most important indicators we can use for significant trend analysis is the direction, or slope, of the 200 period moving average. One of the best opportunities for buying in an early trend is when the slope of the 200 period moving average goes from down to up. In the *TREND*advisor Diamond Analysis, we call this the "transition" point, and it signifies when the market is transitioning to a stronger trending mode (with the other conditions in place). (See Figure 1.6.)

The 50 period moving average describes recent price trend; the 200 period moving average describes longer term price trend. By examining current price in relation to these moving averages, and these moving

The 200 period moving average is a measurement of the long term trend direction.

A ⟶

200 PMA

The calculation is made by adding all closes 1 to 200; the sum is then divided by 200. At Point A we have the result of the calculation.

200 ————————————————————— 1

FIGURE 1.5　Calculating the 200 Period Moving Average
Source: © TradeStation Technologies, Inc. 1991–2005

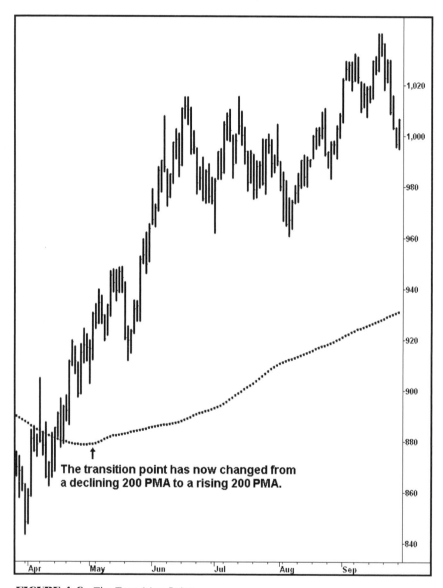

The transition point has now changed from
a declining 200 PMA to a rising 200 PMA.

FIGURE 1.6 The Transition Point
The transition point displays the change in slope of the 200 period moving aver-
age. This signifies when price is potentially transitioning to a different trend.
Source: © TradeStation Technologies, Inc. 1991–2005

averages in relation to each other, we have an excellent toolkit for analyzing trends.

Next, we want tools to measure the strength of the trend, telling us how much price change we are getting over time.

RATE OF CHANGE INDICATOR

The first of these is Rate of Change—trend is price over time. One way of measuring strength of trend is by using the Rate of Change (ROC) indicator. What the Rate of Change indicator measures is how much the price has changed over the lookback period, which is set at 21 periods. We use 21 periods as our length because there are 21 trading days in the month, on average, over a trading year. If the ROC line is rising sharply, this means we are getting strong upward price movement—strong momentum. If the ROC is rising weakly, we do not have strong momentum. On the downside, a sharply falling ROC means there is strong downside price change.

How ROC Is Calculated and What it Is Telling Us

The 21 period Rate of Change indicator is simply the percent of the change in price from the price 21 bars ago. It takes the price of the current bar and divides it by the price of the bar 21 periods ago. This gives a value. If the stock has gone up in the 21 periods, the value will be greater than 1; down, it will be less than 1. This value is then subtracted from one to give the positive change for up periods and negative change for down periods. Finally, this number is multiplied by 100 to give a whole number percentage. For example, in an uptrend, if the current close is 110 and the close 21 bars ago was 100, current close divided by the 21 bars ago close would be 110/100 = 1.10. This value is then subtracted from one (1.10 – 1 = .10) to give a number = .10. Finally, this .10 is multiplied by 100 to give a percent—10 percent. So the ROC value is 10—the stock is up 10 percent. In a downtrend, if the current close is 90 and the close 21 periods ago was 100, 90 divided by 100 equals .9 (90/100 = .9). Point 9 minus 1 equals negative .10 (.9 – 1 = –.10). The –.10 multiplied by 100 equals minus 10 percent so the ROC value is –10, meaning the stock has gone down 10 percent from 21 periods ago. (See Figure 1.7.)

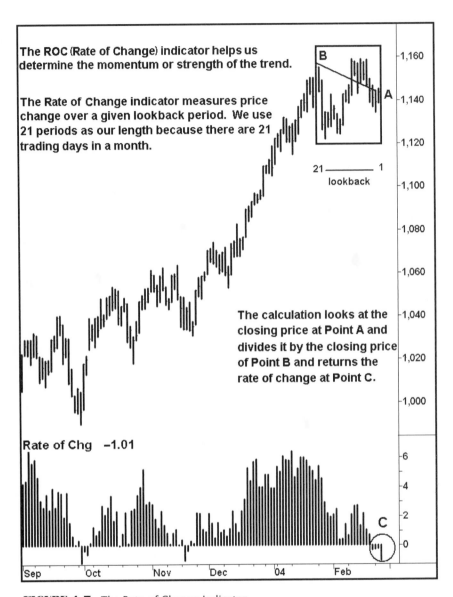

FIGURE 1.7   The Rate of Change Indicator
The ROC (Rate of Change) indicator helps us determine the momentum or strength of the trend.
Source: © TradeStation Technologies, Inc. 1991–2005

STOCHASTICS

Next we use an indicator that tracks closes of price relative to the range they have been in. This is called *stochastics*. What stochastics measure is where the current close is in relation to recent range. If prices are strongly trending, stochastics will give a high reading. This is telling us that current and recent closes are at the upper end of the range—price is high in that range.

How Stochastics Are Calculated and What They Are Telling Us

Stochastics calculate where the close is relative to the recent range. This is accomplished by subtracting the lowest low of the last 21 periods from the current close, then dividing this number by the high of the last 21 periods minus the low of the last 21 periods. In an uptrend, if the current close is 109, and the 21 period high is 110 and the 21 period low is 100, the calculation is 109 minus 100 or 9 (109 − 100 = 9) divided by 110 minus 100 or 10 (110 − 100 = 10). This results in a value of .9 (9/10), which is telling us that the close is at the 90 percent level of the recent range. In a downtrend, if current close is 91, the 21 period low is 90 and the 21 period high is 100, our calculation is 91 − 90 or 1 (91 − 90 = 1) divided by the high of 100 minus the low of 90 or 10 (100 − 90 = 10). This results in a value of .10 (1/10 = .10) or at the 10 percent level of the recent range. The values of these individual calculations for each new close are then averaged over some period (generally 3 bars) to reduce the jumpiness from one calculation to another.

Generally, stocks that are strongly uptrending close high in the range, stocks that are strongly downtrending close low in the range. Stocks that are trendless tend to vacillate from closing low in their range to high in the range.

In our charts in the following chapters, you will see a dotted line on the stochastics indicator, which is drawn at 50 percent. This line cleaves the indicator into two areas. If the stochastics indicator is above 50, this means that the close is in the upper part of the recent range. A reading below 50 means the close is in the lower half of the recent range. As you will see later, where the stochastics readings are is an important part of phase analysis in preparing to trade. (See Figure 1.8.)

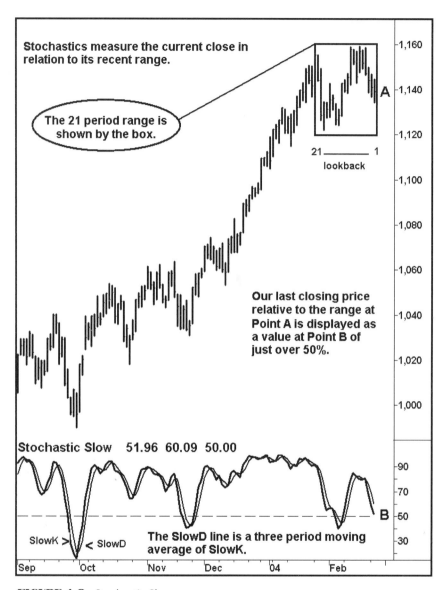

FIGURE 1.8 Stochastic Slow

Stochastic slow measures the current close in relation to its recent range. We use a value of 21 for this calculation. When this indicator is above the 50 dotted line, this shows that the close is in the upper 50 percent of its recent range. When this indicator is below the 50 dotted line, the close is in the lower end of its recent range.

Source: © TradeStation Technologies, Inc. 1991–2005

ACCELERATING VOLUME

One more element of the *TREND*advisor Diamond Analysis is studying volume. The reason we analyze volume is that, as prices increase, we want confirmation that there are increasing transactions at these higher prices. More transactions at higher prices confirm for us that demand is increasing as prices rise. Ideally, we want to see these increases in volume as prices surge (when we are getting higher highs), and decreases in volume as the prices consolidate after the surges.

Volume Oscillator

To analyze volume, we combine a 5 period volume oscillator with a 21 period volume oscillator. The volume oscillator is simply a moving average of volume. We use a moving average of volume to smooth out the spikes of any individual day; this is to reduce the potential for being misled by any one data point. If the short term moving average of volume is surging relative to the longer term, this is telling us we are getting the surge that confirms volume is picking up as the price is moving. (See Figure 1.9.)

THE TOOLKIT

This is our toolkit. For uptrends, the 60 period high/low channel helps us to see when higher highs are occurring, which defines an uptrend. It also helps us to see when there are no more higher highs, which can indicate an end to that trend. The 50 percent retracement line helps us to see if price is in the upper half of the channel (above the line) or the lower half (below the line). The 50 period moving average helps us to see what recent price action has been doing. If the 50 period moving average is sloping up, the market has been moving up. The 200 period moving average helps us to see the longer term trend. If it is moving up, then the longer term trend has been up. The Rate of Change indicator helps us to measure the power, or momentum, of the move. An increasing rate of change signals increasing power on the upside. Stochastics help us to see where closes are happening in relation to the recent range—in uptrends, closes tend to happen at the high end of the range. And the volume oscillator helps us to see if volume is increasing in this trend.

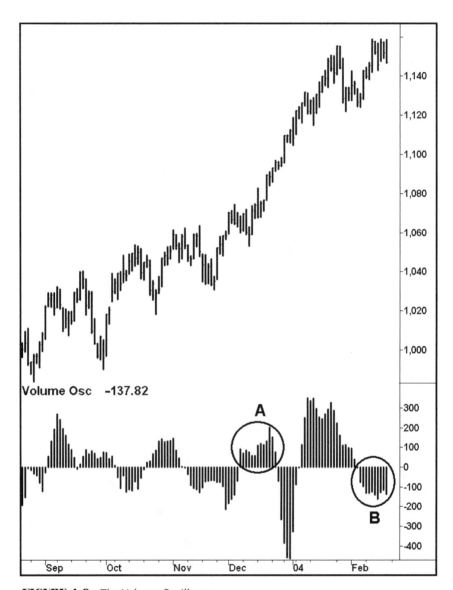

FIGURE 1.9 The Volume Oscillator

The volume oscillator quickly identifies trends in volume. We calculate a 5 period moving average of volume, then subtract this from a 21 period moving average of volume. The result is a value that fluctuates above and below the 0 (zero) line. At Point A we have volume increasing with price moving up, and at Point B we have an absence of volume as price moves to a new high.

Source: © TradeStation Technologies, Inc. 1991–2005

For downtrends, the 60 period low channel helps us to see when lower lows are happening, which defines a downtrend. It also helps us to see when there are no more lower lows, which can indicate an end to that trend. The 50 period moving average helps us to see what recent price action has been doing. If the 50 period moving average is sloping down, the market has been moving down. The 200 period moving average helps us to see the longer-term trend. If it is moving down, then the longer-term trend has been down. The Rate of Change indicator helps us to measure the power, or momentum, of the move, and a sharply dropping rate of change signals increasing power to the downside. Stochastics help us to see where closes are happening in relation to the recent range—generally, in downtrends prices close at the lower end of the range. And the volume oscillator helps us to see if volume is increasing in this trend.

Our toolkit assists us with two things. The first is to analyze trend. It also helps to guide us in making our trading decisions—when to enter, when to exit.

CHAPTER 2

The Six Phases of the *TREND*advisor Diamond

HOW THE DIAMOND METHODOLOGY WORKS

The *TREND*advisor Diamond Methodology aids us in analyzing price behavior as it changes over time. The insights the *TREND*advisor Diamond provides act as a compass for the trader trying to determine price strength or weakness of the financial instrument to be traded. There are six phases of price behavior in the *TREND*advisor Diamond: two clearly trending and four where the trend is less evident, where it could be ending or beginning. The two phases where there is sharpest price movement over time are called "Bullish Phase" for the uptrend and "Bearish Phase" for the downtrend. This chapter will briefly introduce how each of these six phases is defined. We will then examine each phase in more detail, including trading approaches, in the following chapters.

There is an old saying in the market that there will be "a change in momentum before there is a change in direction." If the market has exhibited an expansion of trend over time, a "Bullish Phase" for uptrend, the likelihood of a pullback should unfold. This would show up as a "Warning Phase" in an uptrend that might be signaling the start of what could be the beginning of a countertrend move. If price movement has been downtrending over time, a "Bearish Phase," the chances for a lift should unfold. This would show up as a "Recovery Phase" in a downtrend.

In the progression of market cycles, markets move in a bell curve manner of six parts. In part 1, we begin to see buying interest followed by part 2, acceleration in price and volume. Price then plateaus as the buying interest wanes, part 3, followed by sellers stepping in and beginning

FIGURE 2.1   The *TREND*advisor Diamond
The *TREND*advisor Diamond is broken into two equal and distinct sections. The left side of the Diamond is the "buy side" and the right side is the "sell side." Each side has three phases—the buy side includes the Recovery, Accumulation, and Bullish phases; the sell side includes the Warning, Distribution, and Bearish Phases.

to liquidate long positions, part 4. This sets the stage for an increase in selling activity, part 5, and then price establishes a floor for support, as selling wanes and buyers step in, part 6. Once a base is built, it levels out again, and the cycle repeats itself.

These dynamics are described in the *TREND*advisor Diamond Methodology. The early buying interest is called the Recovery Phase, because it frequently emerges after a downtrend. The step where buying interest becomes more evident is the Accumulation Phase. The accelerating uptrend is the Bullish Phase, which is followed by the Warning Phase, where buying interest has waned. The sellers stepping in is called the Distribution Phase, which leads to the Bearish Phase, where selling interest is intense, followed by a base being built in the Recovery Phase, and the cycle repeats itself.

The *TREND*advisor Diamond Methodology aids us in analyzing price behavior as it changes over time. Markets will cycle between bursts of intense price activity and periods of stability. This natural flow of price expansion and contraction cycles through the six phases. Likewise, markets have times when they are going up and a trader or investor can make money by owning stocks, and times when they are going down, when traders and investors should sell what they own or can make money by shorting stocks. To reflect these dynamics, The *TREND*advisor Diamond is broken into two equal and distinct sections, as shown in Figure 2.1. The left side of the Diamond is the "buy side" and the right side is the "sell side." Each side has three phases—the buy side includes the Recovery, Accumulation, and Bullish phases, the sell side includes the Warning, Distribution, and Bearish Phases.

THE SIX PHASES

The six phases of the Diamond Methodology are defined by three interrelated things: (1) where price is closing in relation to the 50 period moving average; (2) where price is closing in relation to the 200 period moving average; and (3) where the 50 period moving average is in relation to the 200 period moving average.

This is examining where the *current* price (and prices immediately preceding now) is, compared to *recent* price structure embodied in the 50 period simple moving average, and *long term* as the structure captured by the 200 period simple moving average. Putting these parts together leads to precise, specific definitions of price action into these six phases.

Our descriptions will start with the beginning of the phase cycle. This can be compared to the movements that occur in a bell curve. We start with the buy side and cycle to the sell side. For simplicity, we will abbreviate Period Moving Average to PMA.

What defines a phase is where the current price is closing in relation to the moving averages and where the moving averages are in relation to each other. Please note that what the other indicators we described in Chapter 1 are doing has nothing to do with phase definition. For this reason, in this chapter there will be no indicators on the charts except the moving averages.

The Recovery Phase

The Recovery Phase begins as traders who are short decide to cover their positions, and investors decide to buy the stock at its low, as shown in Figure 2.2. Prices begin to stabilize. In the Recovery Phase, the current price action closes above the 50 PMA. What this means is that, currently, prices

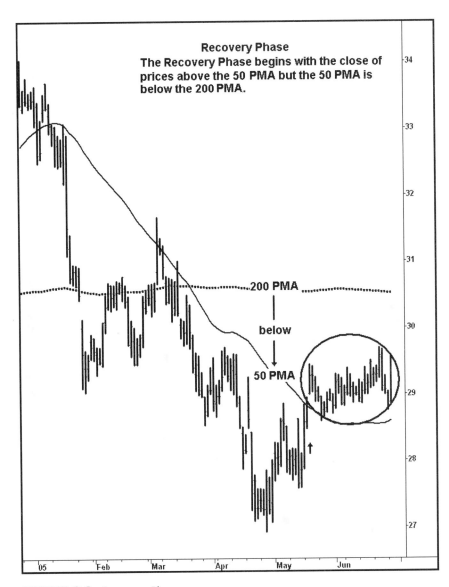

FIGURE 2.2 Recovery Phase
Close > 50 PMA: Close greater than 50 period moving average
Close < 200 PMA: Close less than 200 period moving average
50 PMA < 200 PMA: 50 period moving average less than 200 period moving average
Source: © TradeStation Technologies, Inc. 1991–2005

are stronger than they have been recently, hence they are greater than the 50 PMA. However, the next determinant of the phase is where the price is closing in relation to the 200 period moving average. In the Recovery Phase, price is closing *below* the 200 period moving average. What this means is that even though price is above the 50 PMA, the longer term price action was sufficiently weak that price is still below the 200 PMA. Finally, the third determinant is that the 50 PMA is *below* the 200 PMA. What this means is that the recent price is still below the long term price.

The Recovery Phase begins with the close of the current price above the 50 PMA but less than the 200 PMA, and the relationship of the 50 PMA is less than the 200 PMA. In this price structure, recent and longer term price is weak, but the current price is sufficiently strong to have overcome the recent weakness.

The Accumulation Phase

As more buyers step into the market, the market cycles into the Accumulation Phase. In the Accumulation Phase, investors and traders begin to accumulate positions, and price often moves sideways with a positive bias. (See Figure 2.3.)

As price begins to stabilize or improve, the Accumulation Phase starts with the close of current price above both the 50 PMA and the 200 PMA but the relationship of the 50 PMA is still less than the 200 PMA. In this phase, current price is sufficiently strong to be above recent price and longer term price, but the recent price structure embodied in the 50 PMA has been weak relative to the longer term price structure evidenced by the 200 PMA. Therefore, the Accumulation Phase begins with the close of current price above the 50 PMA and the 200 PMA, but the 50 PMA is still less than the 200 PMA.

The Bullish Phase

The Bullish Phase is frequently where there is substantial buying. (See Figure 2.4.) This phase is defined by the current price closing above both the 50 PMA and the 200 PMA, and the 50 PMA is above the 200 PMA. What this means is that the current price is higher than the recent prices as embodied by the 50 PMA, and that recent price structure is stronger than longer term price structure incorporated in the 200 PMA. I liken the Bullish Phase to going into battle with a full team of soldiers behind you, yielding your best chance of success. To repeat, the Bullish Phase begins with the close of current price above the 50 PMA and the 200 PMA, and the 50 PMA is greater than the 200 PMA.

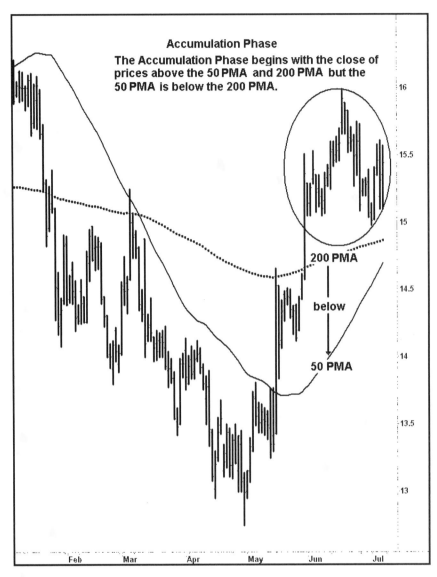

Accumulation Phase

The Accumulation Phase begins with the close of prices above the 50 PMA and 200 PMA but the 50 PMA is below the 200 PMA.

FIGURE 2.3 Accumulation Phase
Close > 50 PMA: Close greater than 50 period moving average
Close > 200 PMA: Close greater than 200 period moving average
50 PMA < 200 PMA: 50 period moving average less than 200 period moving average
Source: © TradeStation Technologies, Inc. 1991–2005

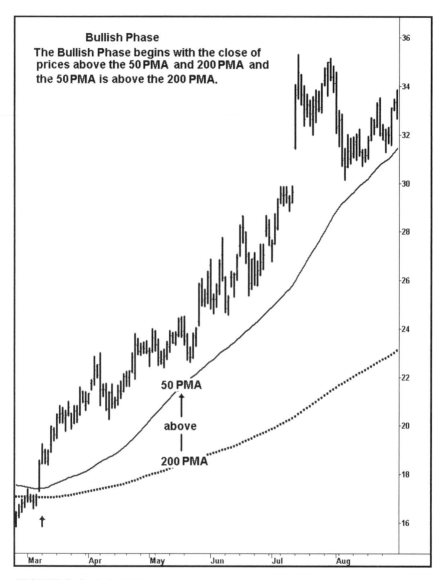

Bullish Phase
The Bullish Phase begins with the close of
prices above the 50 PMA and 200 PMA and
the 50 PMA is above the 200 PMA.

FIGURE 2.4 Bullish Phase
Close > 50 PMA: Close greater than 50 period moving average
Close > 200 PMA: Close greater than 200 period moving average
50 PMA > 200 PMA: 50 period moving average greater than 200 period moving
average
Source: © TradeStation Technologies, Inc. 1991–2005

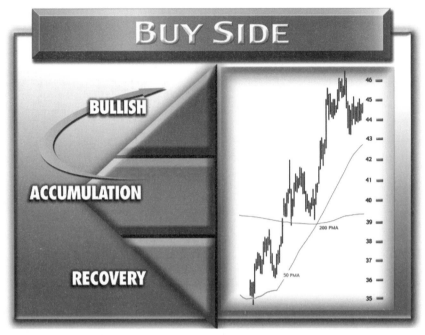

FIGURE 2.5   The Buy Side of the Diamond
The left side of the *TREND*advisor Diamond is the "buy side." It has three phases—
the Recovery, Accumulation, and Bullish phases—which describe the progression
of prices in an uptrend.

These three phases, the Recovery Phase, the Accumulation Phase, and the Bullish Phase, constitute the "buy side" of the *TREND*advisor Diamond, as shown in Figure 2.5. They describe the progression of buying activity that happens in uptrending financial instruments—stocks, mutual funds, commodities, and other futures.

The Warning Phase

The Warning Phase is when buying interest in the stock begins to wane, as shown in Figure 2.6. Price begins to plateau. Traders start taking their profits. The beginning of the Warning Phase is when prices close below the 50 PMA but still above the 200 PMA, and the 50 PMA is above the 200 PMA. What this means is that current price is weaker than recent price, as seen by being below the 50 PMA, but is still stronger than the longer term price of the 200 PMA. Additionally, the recent price of the 50 PMA is still stronger than the longer term price of 200 PMA. These closes below the 50

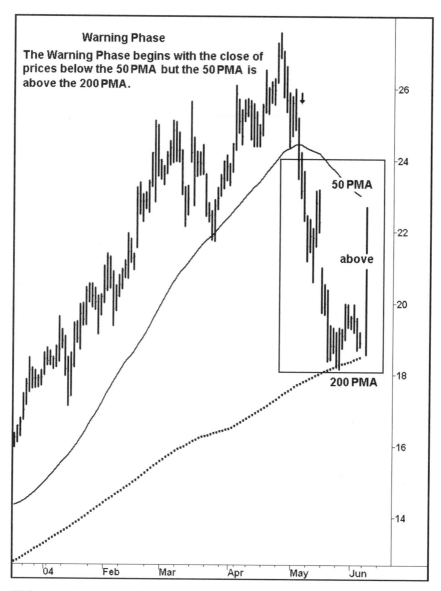

Warning Phase

The Warning Phase begins with the close of prices below the 50 PMA but the 50 PMA is above the 200 PMA.

50 PMA

above

200 PMA

FIGURE 2.6 Warning Phase

Close < 50 PMA: Close less than 50 period moving average

Close > 200 PMA: Close greater than 200 period moving average

50 PMA > 200 PMA: 50 period moving average greater than 200 period moving average

Source: © TradeStation Technologies, Inc. 1991–2005

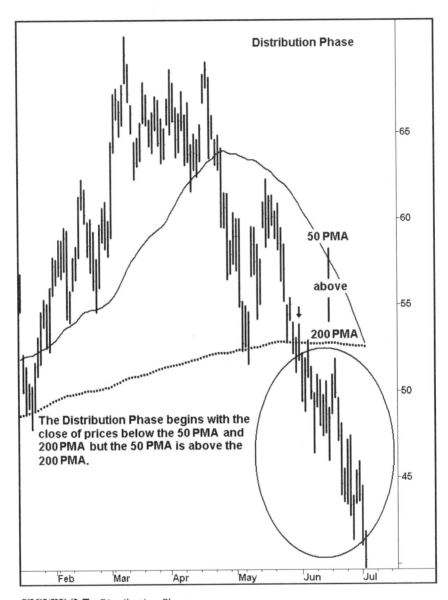

FIGURE 2.7 Distribution Phase

Close < 50 PMA: Close less than 50 period moving average

Close < 200 PMA: Close less than 200 period moving average

50 PMA > 200 PMA: 50 period moving average greater than 200 period moving average

Source: © TradeStation Technologies, Inc. 1991–2005

PMA in an upwardly structured market are signaling a potential end of the uptrend.

The Warning Phase is similar to the top of the bell curve. We now have our current close less than the 50 PMA, but we still have a positive close greater than the 200 PMA, and the relationship of the 50 PMA is greater than the 200 PMA. In this price configuration, current price is weaker than recent prices, but the price structure historically has been relatively strong.

The Distribution Phase

The Distribution Phase is when investors and traders decide to liquidate their holdings, as shown in Figure 2.7. Selling pressure increases. The current price is closing below the 50 PMA and is now also closing below the 200 PMA. However, the 50 PMA is still above the 200 PMA, indicating that even though current price is very weak, recent price has been higher than longer term price.

As price continues to weaken or decline, we now have the current close of price below both the 50 PMA and the 200 PMA, but the relationship of the 50 PMA is still greater than the 200 PMA. In the Distribution Phase, the 50 PMA is still above the 200 PMA, which means that although price is weaker than both averages, there was sufficient recent action high enough for the 50 PMA to still be above the longer term average.

The Bearish Phase

The Bearish Phase is when heightened selling pressure ensues; everyone is selling their stock—both the shorts and investors—which drives prices down sharply over time, as shown in Figure 2.8. This is the weakest of price structures. The current price is closing below both the 50 PMA and the 200 PMA. Additionally, the 50 PMA is now below the 200 PMA. This combination means that current price is weak, and that recent price is weaker than longer term price. We now have the current close less than the 50 PMA and the 200 PMA but, most importantly, the relationship of the 50 PMA is less than the 200 PMA.

These three phases, the Warning Phase, the Distribution Phase, and the Bearish Phase, constitute the "sell side" of the *TREND*advisor Diamond, as shown in Figure 2.9. They describe the progression of selling activity that happens in downtrending financial instruments—stocks, mutual funds, commodities, and other futures.

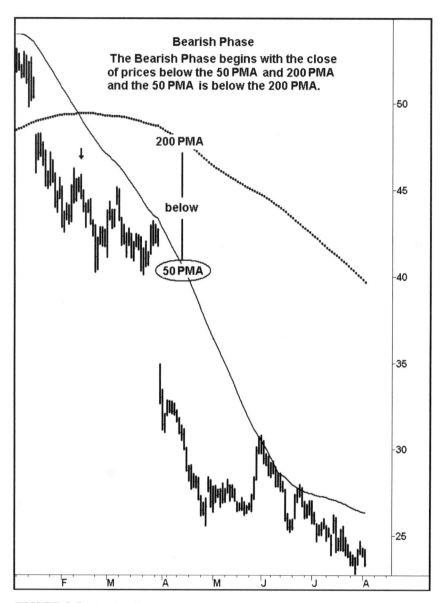

Bearish Phase

The Bearish Phase begins with the close of prices below the 50 PMA and 200 PMA and the 50 PMA is below the 200 PMA.

200 PMA

below

50 PMA

FIGURE 2.8 Bearish Phase
Close < 50 PMA: Close less than 50 period moving average
Close < 200 PMA: Close less than 200 period moving average
50 PMA < 200 PMA: 50 period moving average less than 200 period moving average
Source: © TradeStation Technologies, Inc. 1991–2005

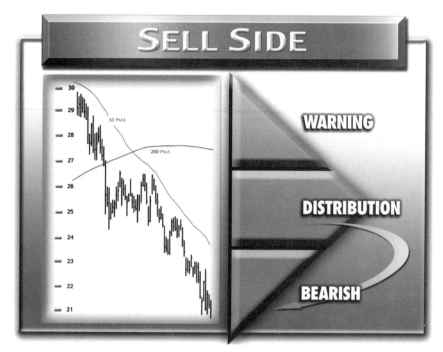

FIGURE 2.9 The Sell Side of the Diamond
The right side of the *TREND*advisor Diamond is the "sell side." It has three phases—
the Warning, Distribution, and Bearish phases—which describe the progression of
prices in a downtrend.

SUMMARY

There you have it! We now can define all price activity into six phases. As
you can see, each phase characterizes the trading dynamics that underlie
it. This means that each phase has its own distinct patterns and, therefore,
trading each phase needs its own separate approach.

Because each phase has individual price dynamics, the various indicators we use will behave differently in each phase. This means that we have
to interpret what the indicators are telling us based on which phase the
stock is in.

In the following chapters, we will more fully explore each of these
phases and consider how to approach trading them.

CHAPTER 3

The Recovery Phase

The Recovery Phase occurs as traders who are short decide to cover their positions, and investors decide to nibble while the stock is near its low. Prices begin to stabilize, usually after some kind of long decline. To review: the Recovery Phase begins with the close of current price above the 50 PMA, but the close is less than the 200 PMA, and the relationship of the 50 PMA is less than the 200 PMA. (See Figure 3.1.) In this price structure, recent (50 PMA) and longer term (200 PMA) prices are weak, but the current price is sufficiently strong to have overcome the recent weakness. In this phase, there frequently are no new lows in the price channel, and the 50 PMA is losing (or has lost) its downward slope.

TRADING DYNAMICS OF THE RECOVERY PHASE

Every price that happens reflects the matching of a buyer with a seller. The progression of how prices behave over time gives us insights into the dynamics of the changing nature of the forces of supply and demand—the forces of buyers and sellers interacting.

For every price that accomplishes a sale, there must be a buyer and a seller. If there are buyers but no sellers, prices have to rise until sellers are induced to sell. Likewise, if there are sellers but no buyers, then prices must fall until buyers are induced into buying. For the purpose of the following discussion, think of buyers as demand and sellers as supply. If demand outstrips supply—if there are more buyers than sell-

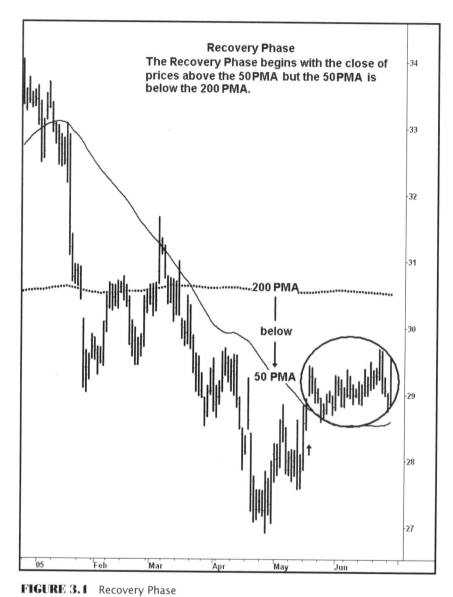

FIGURE 3.1 Recovery Phase
Source: © TradeStation Technologies, Inc. 1991–2005

ers—prices will rise until sellers have an incentive to sell, thus increasing supply to meet demand. If supply overwhelms demand—that is, if there are more would-be sellers than buyers—then prices must fall until they become sufficiently cheap for buyers to step in, or demand to pick up to meet supply.

In the context of supply and demand, in order for prices to be rising one of several things may be happening. One possibility is that demand is staying the same but supply is going down—if there are the same numbers of buyers for something but supply drops, then price will rise (a hurricane shuts down oil production). If demand is increasing but supply stays the same, again prices will rise.

- Prices rising can be caused by demand staying the same but supply decreasing.
- Prices rising can also be caused by demand increasing but supply staying the same.
- If prices are going sideways, then demand and supply are in balance.

In the Recovery Phase, generally selling pressure is drying up—there are no more sellers to sell. This means that supply has dried up. While prices were going down, there were plenty of sellers willing to dump shares on the market. These sellers included both those who were "long and wrong" and wanted out, as well as the short sellers who profit from declining prices. However, as prices start to flatten out, several things start happening.

Who is willing to buy as prices are plunging? In the stock market, there are two primary forces. The first of these is the value-oriented investors. Value investors buy things when they are cheap. The more a price drops, the closer it gets to where someone will find it a bargain. If a stock has been falling as the result of a decline in the business—fewer sales, less profits—eventually that price drops to a level where the value is so compelling that buyers will step in. (Warren Buffett's purchases in the bear market of the early 1970s were a classic value purchase.)

As prices start to stabilize, a second factor kicks in. Remember our discussion about the short sellers, those who make money when the market is declining? What do they have to do to capture their profits? They have to buy, which is called covering their shorts. They don't want to buy while prices are still declining, because they make more money as the price continues down. However, when prices start going sideways for a period of time, they no longer make additional profits. In order to capture their profits, they have to buy.

Additionally, as prices start to stabilize, the sophisticated traders, those in the markets every day, start buying. The more prices go sideways, the more likely there will be traders buying on dips toward the lows. This is what creates a level of support in the market—support levels being places where buyers appear and prices no longer decline. However, although supply is drying up in the Recovery Phase and the professional traders—hedge funds and the like—are buying the dips toward support, these professional traders are also willing to sell the short term rallies that occur early in the Recovery Phase. The reason for this is that there are defined resistance levels, levels where sellers on the preceding declines were willing to sell. Early in the Recovery Phase, these resistance levels bring out the short-term traders who are taking their profits from the purchases on the dips toward support. These short-term traders may also be selling short on these weak rallies, and then covering the shorts as prices pull back toward support. This trading dynamic is what creates a series of lows in the Recovery Phase and a narrowing of the 60 period high/low channel (more about this later in this chapter).

In short, in the Recovery Phase selling pressure is abating because there is no one left to sell. Buying interest is appearing. This buying interest may include short covering.

IDENTIFYING POTENTIAL TRADING CANDIDATES IN THE RECOVERY PHASE

There are several characteristics that stocks will exhibit if they are potential Recovery Phase trading candidates. Stocks that do not meet these criteria do not qualify. We are training your eye to see what good potential candidates look like.

In the Recovery Phase, the 60 period low indicator is frequently indicating no new lows by being flat for some time. This is telling us that there have been no new lows recently. The 60 period high indicator frequently declines, or flattens, meaning there have been no new highs for some time, or the highs have been declining (typical of a downtrend). Because a downtrend is defined as a series of lower lows with lower highs in between, the absence of new lows in the 60 period channel is the best evidence of the downtrend potentially ending.

Look for the following characteristics in our indicators in the Recovery Phase to identify potential trading candidates.

60 Period High/Low Channel

In the Recovery Phase, frequently there are no new lows in the 60 period high/low channel. The high channel is frequently dropping, caused by the lower highs in the preceding price action. (See Figure 3.2.) The compression,

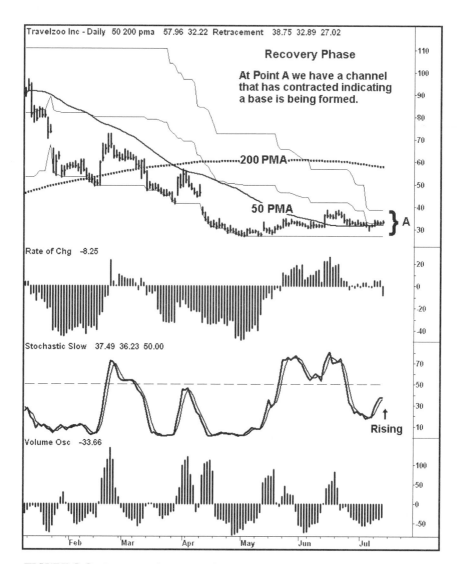

FIGURE 3.2 Recovery Phase: Travelzoo, Inc.
In the Recovery Phase a channel that has contracted is providing us with a clue that
a horizontal base is being formed. A flat or rising 50 PMA shows stabilizing current
prices, while a rising stochastic suggests current price relative to its range is moving up.
Source: © TradeStation Technologies, Inc. 1991–2005

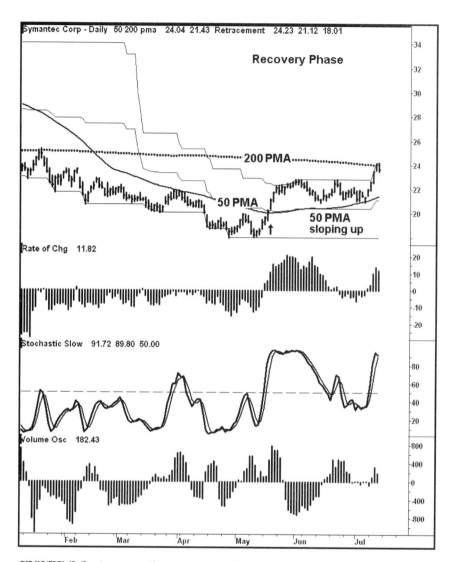

FIGURE 3.3 Recovery Phase: Symantec Corp.

The stage is set for an advance with price crossing above the upward sloping 50 PMA (see the up arrow showing where the Recovery Phase begins). The next bar confirms the move as price closes above the 50 percent retracement area, rate of change is positive, stochastics are above the 50 zone, and the volume oscillator is above zero.

Source: © TradeStation Technologies, Inc. 1991–2005

or narrowing of the 60 period high/low channel, captures the sideways price action that occurs at bottoms.

50 and 200 Period Moving Average

In the Recovery Phase, the close is above the 50 Period Moving Average as seen in Figure 3.3. Frequently, the 50 PMA has lost its downward slope, or is flattening out. A flat 50 PMA means that, on average, prices are not changing much. This is also indicative of prices "recovering" after a long decline. In the Recovery Phase, the close is still below the 200 PMA and the 50 PMA is also below the 200 PMA. The close below the 200 PMA means that prices are still unable to exceed the longer term, downward price trend. The longer the recovery phase goes on, the more likely the 200 PMA will flatten out and lose its downward slope. If the recovery phase is fairly short in duration, and the slope of the 200 is still sharply down, the likelihood is that the stock needs more time to recover from its downtrend.

Rate of Change Indicator

In the Recovery Phase the Rate of Change indicator is starting to become positive and to flatten out, as shown in Figure 3.4. This is caused by the sideways price action, which means that prices are wafting slightly up and down, not fiercely up and down. The ROC values are smaller and generally more positive. If price starts moving sharply up, the ROC indicator will become much more positive.

Stochastics

When stocks enter the Recovery Phase, they frequently have been going sideways for some time. This means the part of the stochastics indicator that measures the recent range will be narrowing. As prices start to advance, the closes will be high in that range—this will lead to persistently high stochastics readings above the 50 percent mark. In Figure 3.5, note that at point B and after it the 21 period range part of the stochastics calculation is expanding because the higher prices are creating new highs of the range (see Chapter 1 for a discussion of how stochastics are calculated).

Volume Oscillator

Preceding the Recovery Phase, there may be little interest in the stock—prices have been drifting around or going down. When the stock enters

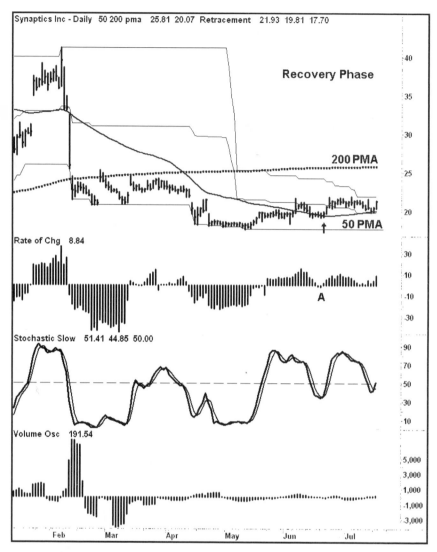

FIGURE 3.4 Recovery Phase: Synaptics, Inc.
At point A the rate of change indicator has moved back into positive ground after a slight decline when the Recovery Phase begins (see the up arrow). Future price activity looks promising with the 50 PMA now sloping to the upside. Note that the 200 PMA is also still sloping up. Stochastics have also broken above the 50 zone with the volume oscillator moving into positive territory.
Source: © TradeStation Technologies, Inc. 1991–2005

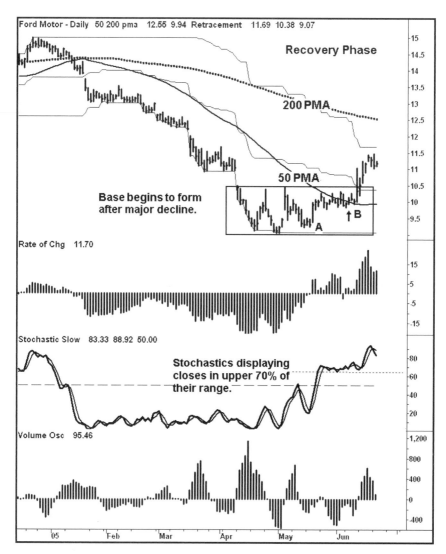

FIGURE 3.5 Recovery Phase: Ford Motor Company
After a major decline, base building takes place as price begins to make higher
lows at points A & B (the Recovery Phase begins where the up arrow is pointing at
B). After several months of base building, price has been closing in the upper end
of its range. This is displaying a stochastics value not only above the 50 percent
level but also above the 70 percent level.
Source: © TradeStation Technologies, Inc. 1991–2005

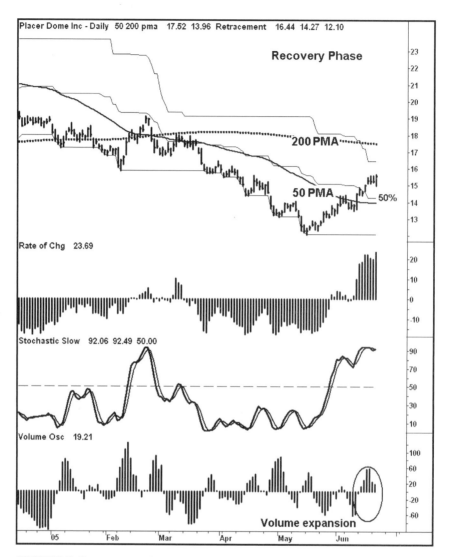

FIGURE 3.6   Recovery Phase: Placer Dome, Inc.
After a steep decline PDG begins to recover with price penetrating the 50 percent retracement area with an increase in volume. Note that the volume oscillator surges as price has rallied. Momentum based on the Rate of Change indicator has also reversed, while stochastics are clearly above the 50 zone.
Source: © TradeStation Technologies, Inc. 1991–2005

the Recovery Phase, we want to see that there is buying interest in the stock. (See Figure 3.6.) If there is buying interest, there will be an increase in volume—more transactions happening at those higher prices. Therefore, we want to see the volume oscillator turn positive as the prices rise. For trading and investing, *if* prices are rising and volume (supply) is going up, then demand *must* be outstripping supply. This is why we look at volume—to confirm this dynamic. If there is no surge in volume, and prices are drifting around, then there is equilibrium in the instrument. Supply and demand are in balance—buying pressure and selling pressure are equal (see the volume oscillator in Figure 3.4 for an example of equilibrium).

THE IDEAL RECOVERY PHASE CHARACTERISTICS

The best looking Recovery Phase charts will have the characteristics in the following list. If these conditions are present, the likelihood of positive phase progression is higher.

Buy Side	**Recovery Phase**
50 PMA	Flat to sloping up
200 PMA	Sloping down
50% Retracement	Price at or above
60 period higher highs	Not required
60 period higher lows	Not required but better if sideways
Rate of Change	Begins to turn positive
Stochastic	Starts to climb above the 50 zone
Volume oscillator	Above zero on the rallies

The Ideal Recovery Phase Chart

Figure 3.7 illustrates the components of the ideal Recovery Phase chart.

Weekly Recovery Phase Chart

The *TREND*advisor Diamond Analysis works on different time frames, which makes it useful to a broad range of both traders and investors. For example, doing analysis on a weekly basis can be more appropriate for longer-term investors (like portfolio managers) who want to see the underlying trend. This is illustrated in Figure 3.8. Note that the longer the time frame, the more lag there will be in seeing trends materialize. Conversely, the shorter the time frame, the more responsive the indicators are

The Ideal Recovery Phase Chart

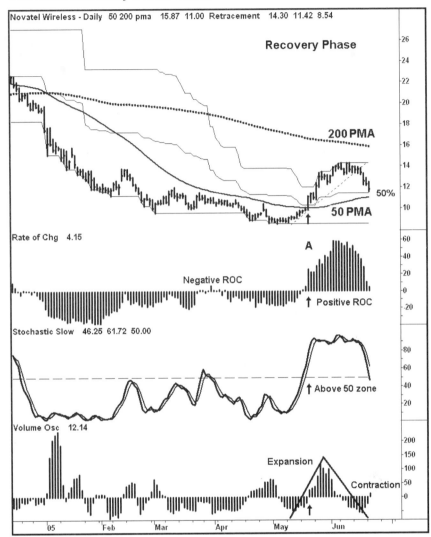

FIGURE 3.7 Recovery Phase: Novatel Wireless, Inc.
Components of the ideal Recovery Phase chart would be: at point A price crosses above the 50 PMA, placing NVTL in the Recovery Phase. With this positive close, the 50 PMA slope turns positive as we move above the 50 percent retracement of the 60 period channel. The momentum Rate of Change has transitioned from negative to positive, and stochastics are clearly above the 50 zone. Also, as price moved into the Recovery Phase, there was an expansion of volume. On the slight pullback that followed (far right on the chart), there was a contraction in volume.
Source: © TradeStation Technologies, Inc. 1991–2005

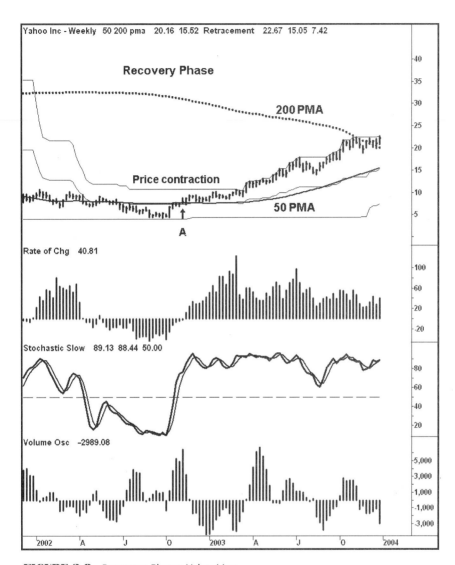

Yahoo Inc - Weekly 50 200 pma   20.16 15.52 Retracement   22.67 15.05 7.42

Recovery Phase

200 PMA

Price contraction

50 PMA

A

Rate of Chg   40.81

Stochastic Slow   89.13 88.44 50.00

Volume Osc   −2989.08

FIGURE 3.8 Recovery Phase: Yahoo! Inc.
The weekly chart of YHOO shows price contraction for over one year as seen in the 60 period high/low channel. At point A, YHOO enters the Recovery Phase by price crossing above the 50 PMA. Additionally, it is crossing above the 50 percent retracement area. This sets the stage for further price expansion. Later, the 50 PMA begins its upward slope, price begins to make higher highs, the ROC indicator is positive, and stochastics are persistently above the 50 zone.
Source: © TradeStation Technologies, Inc. 1991–2005

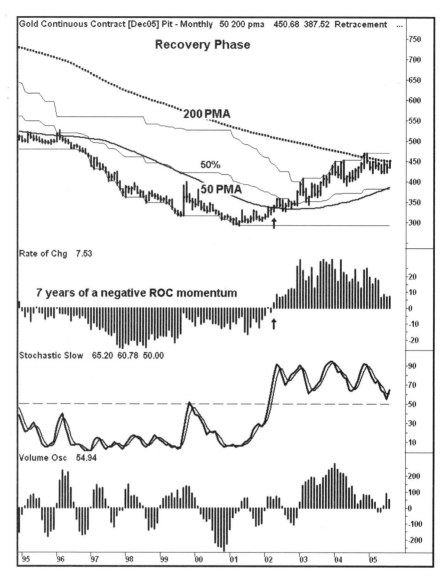

FIGURE 3.9 Recovery Phase: Gold
The monthly chart of gold had seen 84 months of negative momentum. Also, stochastic had been below the 50 zone for approximately the same period. In 2002 a shift occurred. Price crossed above the 50 PMA, putting gold into the Recovery Phase (see up arrow). Then the 50 PMA began to flatten, often a first sign of a trend change. At the up arrow, when gold entered the Recovery Phase, the ROC indicator moved into positive territory. Stochastics above the 50 zone show that price is persistently closing higher.
Source: © TradeStation Technologies, Inc. 1991–2005

to emerging trend. Longer time frames are used by the big mutual fund complexes that do technical analysis. They do not want to respond to every blip in the market because their size makes it impossible to quickly get in or out of positions. That is why they use weekly charts—the longer time frame charts have less price volatility.

Commodity: Monthly Recovery Phase Chart

The *TREND*advisor Diamond Analysis also works on different financial instruments, especially on those where there are sophisticated participants with different objectives. For example, the following monthly chart of gold shows the change in the underlying trend, as illustrated in Figure 3.9. The longer the time frame, the more lag there is in seeing trends materialize. Conversely, in a shorter time frame, the indicators are more likely to show an emerging trend. Longer time frames are what the biggest players that do technical analysis use. They don't respond to every blip in the market—their size makes it impossible to get in or out of positions quickly. Those who are looking for long term trends use longer term time frame analysis. They give up being in at the very bottom and being out at the very top in an attempt to stick with major trends of long duration.

Mutual Fund: Weekly Recovery Phase Chart

As we have seen in the preceding charts, The *TREND*advisor Diamond Analysis works on different instruments, which means both short term traders and long term investors can use it. Figure 3.10 shows the Recovery Phase analysis as applied to a widely held mutual fund. Please note that there is no volume indictor for mutual funds because daily inflows and outflows change the amount in the pool of money in the fund. This is different from stocks and other financial instruments that have a fixed number of shares that change hands.

TRADING THE RECOVERY PHASE

When a market or stock first enters the Recovery Phase by crossing above the 50 PMA, this is frequently an early indication that the preceding downward price action could be coming to an end. The Recovery Phase is the first phase on the "buy side" of the *TREND*advisor Diamond. It is a phase to consider for establishing new long positions because entry prices are generally low. The more trading criteria from the *TREND*advisor Diamond

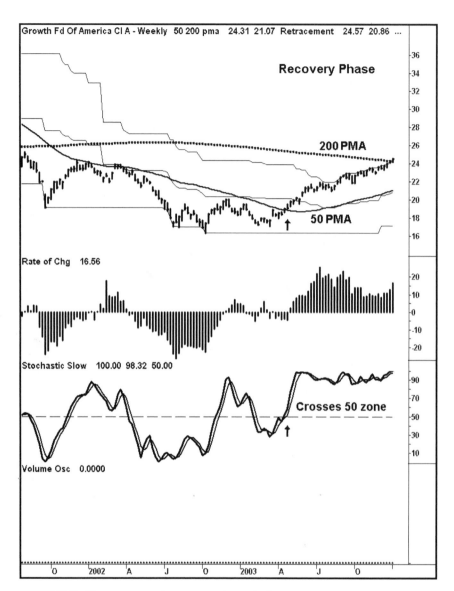

FIGURE 3.10 Recovery Phase: Growth Fund of America

The weekly chart of the Growth Fund of America provided a clue to the end of the downward trend by making a higher low at the beginning of 2003. When price crossed above the 50 PMA, placing AGTHX into the Recovery Phase, we began to see signs of a flattening 50 PMA. The ROC and stochastic moved above their respective levels, adding to the break above the 50 percent retracement area and making a further move toward a higher high in the 60 period channel.

Source: © TradeStation Technologies, Inc. 1991–2005

Matrix that the chart exhibits, the better the chances a long trade may succeed (see the earlier Ideal Recovery Phase Chart). However, the chances that the stock rockets straight up are slim. Therefore, buying (establishing a new long position) early in a Recovery Phase is unwise for two reasons. The first is that the probability of success is low—remember that even though current price is up, more recent price structure in the 50 PMA and longer term price structure in the 200 PMA are down. The trend is still down. So to buy (go long) is to be fighting the more significant trend, which could resume and result in the buyer taking a loss. The second reason to avoid going long early in a recovery phase is the time it takes to make a return on the money invested. It takes time for a stock to recover from a downtrend. If we buy a stock early in the Recovery Phase, capital is tied up in something that is unlikely to earn a decent return for a while. To summarize, the risk is high and the likely return is low—not a good formula for success.

However, if we have been short the market or a particular stock, the beginning of the Recovery Phase could be an excellent alert that we must prepare to exit the short.

Before we talk about guidelines for trading the Recovery Phase, let's talk about some basic principles of capital allocation in a portfolio. Your capital should be divided into parts so that you are diversified across a number of positions. *Never* put all your capital into any one position. Professional money managers are usually diversified across 10 or 20 positions at a minimum, and frequently more. The fewer positions you have, the more concentrated you are, which usually means more risk. The more positions, the more diversified you are, which means less risk. For that reason, you also should be well diversified. For illustration purposes only, suppose you conclude that to be well diversified you should have 20 portfolio positions. This means the full amount of capital you have to allocate to each position is 1/20th of your portfolio. If you have $100,000, your capital for any one normal position would be $5,000.

Trading tactics for this phase might include:

1. If you are going to establish new long positions in the Recovery Phase, use 1/3 the capital of what would be your usual, normal position size. This does two things. First, a smaller position size means you will have less capital at risk if the stock goes against you and you get stopped out. Second, you will have less capital tied up in something that may take time to produce profits.

2. *Always* have a stop. Your stop should be a logical place on the chart where the trade is clearly failing—for long positions, this could include a close below the 50 PMA, which would constitute a phase failure.

3. The longer the Recovery Phase goes on, the more evidence you will have of how it is likely to resolve. If you look at Figures 3.2, 3.3, 3.4, 3.7, and 3.8, you will see that after these stocks first entered the Recovery Phase, even if they rallied initially, they eventually consolidated before advancing again. Waiting for more evidence before entering a long in the Recovery Phase is wise, because, as time goes on, more of the criteria for an Ideal Recovery Phase are met. Particularly, look for the 50 PMA to be flat when the phase begins, and sloping up as the phase matures. Price should be at or above the 50 percent retracement line of the 60 period high/low channel. The Rate of Change indicator begins to turn positive and stochastics start to climb above the 50 zone. The volume oscillator crosses above zero, particularly on rallies, thus indicating a pickup in volume.

4. *Always* have a plan to capture profits. At *TREND*advisor, we harvest part of the trade when it hits the first profit target, and then raise our stop on the remaining portion to the entry price. By using this as our methodology, we book profits on part of our position. For the remaining part, we protect ourselves from a loss by setting the stop at breakeven, while allowing for additional profits if the stock continues to advance.

5. If you are holding a short position that enters the Recovery Phase, start to book profits in the Recovery Phase by reducing your short position. The longer the stock has been in a basing pattern, the flatter the direction of the moving averages, and the closer the flattening moving averages are to converging, the more you should aggressively cover your shorts. Just as important, be certain to refine the exit strategy for your remaining short position.

THE END OF THE RECOVERY PHASE

Part of our job as traders is to be vigilant to the end of trends that we are trading. The Recovery Phase will end in one of two ways. It will either transition into the next positive phase or it will fail, with a close back below the 50 PMA.

A transition into the next positive phase (the Accumulation Phase) is covered in Chapter 4, and it is the best outcome for a Recovery Phase trade. However, as traders and investors, we have to be aware that some of our trades will not work out. Our approach is to accept the reality that some things will not work and prepare you so you can identify what that looks like. Being prepared, knowing what to look for if something is not

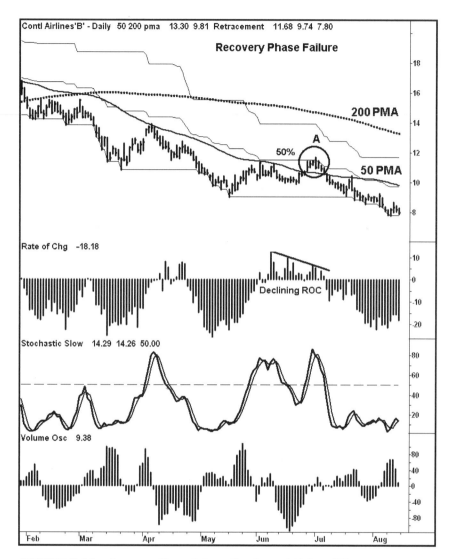

FIGURE 3.11 Recovery Phase Failure: Continental Airlines "B"
The Recovery Phase failure is often seen after steep price declines. The first pull up into the phase frequently meets with failure. Failure is more likely if the price rallies above a declining 50 PMA and is halted at the lower side of the 50 percent retracement of the 60 period channel. Also note that the 200 PMA is sloping down, and the 50 PMA is far below it, which signifies that there has not been sufficient time for the downtrend to consolidate.
Source: © TradeStation Technologies, Inc. 1991–2005

working, will help you to act. Too many of the traders and investors we work with show up with no understanding of what to do when things go against them, and get paralyzed into inaction. This exacerbates losses. It is far better to realize, and be prepared, that some things will not work, and to look for the signs of a Recovery Phase failure, and have in your trading plan the action steps you will take if it materializes.

RECOVERY PHASE FAILURE CHART

It is not unusual for a stock to fail after it enters the Recovery Phase for the first time, as shown in Figure 3.11 on previous page. If the price falls back below the 50 PMA, this means the phase has failed. A Recovery Phase failure is more likely if the 50 PMA is sloping down (price is fighting the recent trend); the price is in the lower half of the price channel (at or below the declining 50 percent retracement line); and the ROC is small (indicating very little positive momentum) or negative. Stochastics may briefly rise above 50, indicating that closes are in the upper region of the recent range, but there will be resistance there, and stochastics will quickly drop back down. There is no surge in volume. The lack of volume on the rally means there is little buying interest in the stock even though the price has risen.

CHAPTER 4

The Accumulation Phase

Coming after the Recovery Phase, the Accumulation Phase is where investors and traders begin to accumulate positions (see Figure 4.1). Price often moves sideways with a positive bias.

As price begins to stabilize or improve, current price now closes above both the 50 PMA and the 200 PMA, but the relationship of the 50 PMA is still less than the 200 PMA. This defines the Accumulation Phase. Current price is sufficiently strong to be above recent price and longer term price, but the recent price structure has been weak relative to the longer term price structure. There are frequently new highs in the 60 period channel, the slope of the 50 PMA is upward, and the 200 PMA is losing or has lost its downward slope.

TRADING DYNAMICS OF THE ACCUMULATION PHASE

It is the progression of how prices behave over time that gives us insights into the dynamics of the changing nature of the forces of supply and demand—the forces of buyers and sellers interacting. The Accumulation Phase characterizes demand increasing. Please review the detailed discussion about the dynamics of supply and demand in Chapter 3. In summary: for every price that happens, there must be a buyer (creating demand) and a seller (creating supply). If there are buyers but no sellers, prices have to rise until sellers are induced to sell. If there are sellers but no buyers, then prices must fall until buyers are induced into buying.

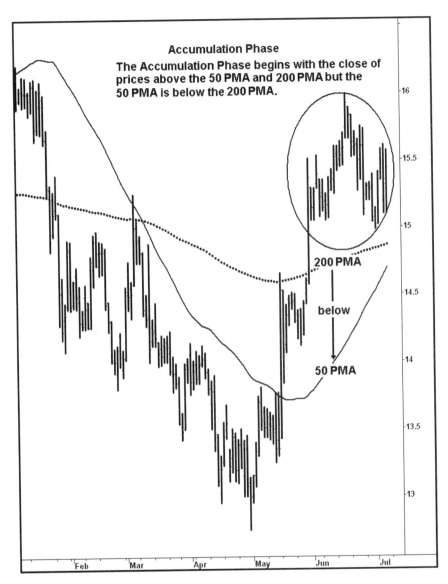

FIGURE 4.1   Accumulation Phase
Source: © TradeStation Technologies, Inc. 1991–2005

In the Accumulation Phase, with rising prices, one of several things must be happening. One possibility is that demand is staying the same, but supply is going down—if there are the same numbers of buyers for something but supply drops (a hurricane shuts down oil production), then prices will rise. If demand is increasing but supply stays the same, then prices will rise as well.

- Prices rising can be caused by demand staying the same but supply decreasing.
- Prices rising can also be caused by demand increasing but supply staying the same.
- Prices rising can also be caused by demand rising faster than supply.
- If prices are going sideways, then demand and supply are in balance.

In the Accumulation Phase, what is generally going on is that buying pressure is rising. After a long period of consolidation and a series of rallies, there now is more urgent buying. As prices start to rally, several things start happening.

First, investors (mutual fund portfolio managers and other professional investors) are increasingly convinced that they should own this instrument. If it is a stock, whatever the problems were that caused the previous sell off are being solved. Investors are much more willing to buy in anticipation of better earnings. The Accumulation Phase shows increasing confidence in the stock. If it is a commodity, there is a change in the underlying dynamics of demand, or something is happening that may lead to a drop in supply (drought conditions forecast in the Midwest) or a pickup in demand (rising beef purchases because of the popularity of the low carbohydrate diet craze).

As prices rally, a second factor kicks in. Remember our discussion about the short sellers, who make money when the market is declining? What do they have to do to capture their profits? They have to buy, which is called covering their shorts. They don't want to buy while prices are still declining, because they are making more money as the price continues down. However, when prices start going sideways for a period of time, they are no longer making additional profits. In order to capture their profits, they have to buy. With prices rallying, their profits are quickly disappearing so they now are more eager to buy. If they don't, their profits continue to evaporate as prices rise, which reduces their paychecks because they are paid only on what they make in profits.

Additionally, with prices rallying, the sophisticated traders, those in the markets every day, increase their buying. The more prices rally, creating an uptrend, the more likely there will be traders buying breakouts at new highs. These traders are much less likely to be selling during rallies, which would constrain price (although they may sell in the very short term and quickly buy back on the consolidation. This is what causes a series of higher lows in the Accumulation Phase). Traders are much more likely to be buying, creating underlying demand. In short, in the Accumulation Phase, buying pressure is increasing. As you can see, there are several groups who are starting to compete in purchasing—this is what causes prices to rise. There are fewer groups willing to sell.

IDENTIFYING POTENTIAL TRADING CANDIDATES IN THE ACCUMULATION PHASE

There are several characteristics that stocks will exhibit if they are potential Accumulation Phase trading candidates. Stocks that do not meet these criteria do not qualify to be potential candidates. We are training your eye to see what good potential candidates look like.

In the Accumulation Phase, the 60 period low indicator is frequently indicating no new lows by being flat for some time. This is telling us that there have been no new lows recently. At the beginning of the Accumulation Phase, the 60 period high indicator is frequently declining, or flattening, meaning there also have been no new highs for some time. However, as the Accumulation Phase progresses, it is not unusual for the price to press against the high channel, particularly after long periods of basing. If the basing period has been extensive, rallies later on in the Accumulation Phase will lead to new highs in the 60 period high/low channel.

Look for the characteristics described in the next five sections as indicators in the Accumulation Phase that will identify potential trading candidates.

60 Period High/Low Channel

In the Accumulation Phase, frequently there are no new lows in the 60 period high/low channel. The high channel (see Figure 4.2) is frequently expanding, caused by the higher highs in the price action. An uptrend is defined as a series of higher highs. The expanding high channel shows this. When the uptrend becomes firmly established with a series of new price highs, the sophisticated traders in hedge funds and trading desks become more aggressive in their buying. This is part of what fuels further price increases.

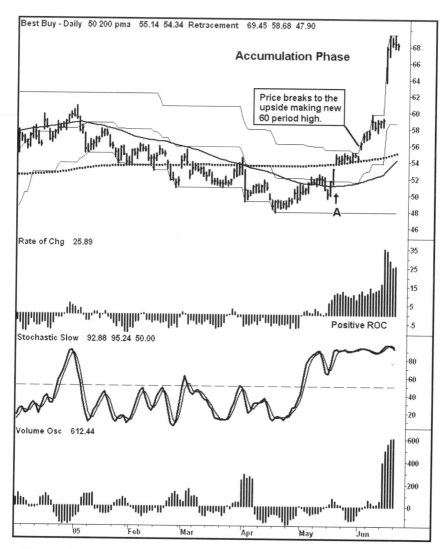

FIGURE 4.2 Accumulation Phase: Best Buy Co., Inc.

At point A, BBY enters the Accumulation Phase by price crossing above the 200 PMA (see up arrow). Additionally, price above the 50 percent retracement of the 60 period channel further confirms buying interest. After trading sideways for a couple of weeks, price expands to the upside by making new highs in the 60 period high/low channel. These new highs define an uptrend, showing the increase in demand that is typical of the Accumulation Phase.

Source: © TradeStation Technologies, Inc. 1991–2005

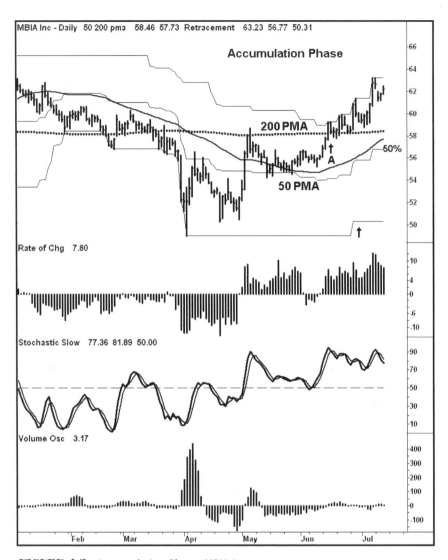

FIGURE 4.3 Accumulation Phase: MBIA Inc.

At point A price makes its way into the Accumulation Phase with a close above the 200 PMA (see up arrow at A). The long term moving average (200 PMA), which has been flat, develops a slight upward bias. This coupled with a new 60 period high and a higher 60 period low (see up arrow under the rising 60 period low channel) bodes well for a continuation of the uptrend.

Source: © TradeStation Technologies, Inc. 1991–2005

50 and 200 Period Moving Average

In the Accumulation Phase, the close is above both the 50 and the 200 period moving averages. The 50 PMA should be rising—a rising PMA means that the recent trend has turned upward, as shown in Figure 4.3. If the 200 PMA is flat or rising slightly, this means that price has been going sideways, on average, for some time, which indicates a long basing pattern. Higher prices will quickly kick that average positive. Price is now also above the 200 period moving average. This means that price has been sufficiently strong to overcome the longer term downtrend. Frequently, the 200 PMA will be flattening out, signifying that the longer term price action has been moving sideways for some time. In an Accumulation Phase that represents a long basing pattern, the 50 PMA and the 200 PMA will be converging. This setup is much better than an Accumulation Phase where the 200 PMA is still sharply sloping down and the 50 PMA is far below the 200 PMA. In that circumstance, the price has moved sharply higher but is more likely to fall than if the moving averages have converged and price has been in a long period of contraction.

Rate of Change Indicator

In the Accumulation Phase, prices are beginning to accelerate. This means that the Rate of Change indicator will be positive, as shown in Figure 4.4. It also should be surging, showing that price has increased substantially from 21 periods ago.

Stochastics

In the Accumulation Phase, as prices break out to the upside, the range is expanding. In uptrending markets, prices tend to close at the high end of their range (see Figure 4.5). This will lead to persistently high stochastics readings, above the 50 percent zone (to review how stochastics are calculated, please see the section in Chapter 1).

Volume Oscillator

In the Accumulation Phase, we want to see rallies accompanied by surges in volume. If volume increases while prices are rising, this means that demand is outstripping supply—more transactions are happening at the higher prices. The volume oscillator will jump sharply, which shows that the 5 period moving average of volume is rising quickly over the

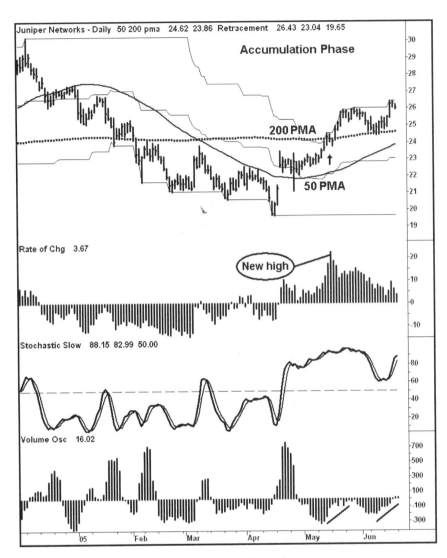

FIGURE 4.4 Accumulation Phase: Juniper Networks

JNPR enters the Accumulation Phase when price crosses above the 200 PMA. Almost immediately thereafter, the uptrend commences when price penetrates the overhead resistance, making a new high in the 60 period high/low channel. The ROC indicator makes a new high, showing the significant recent price increases from 21 periods ago (about 20 percent! In three weeks!). Note that both moving averages are sloping up—the trend of recent price in the 50 PMA and the longer-term price in the 200 PMA is up. Stochastics are clearly above the 50 zone. Volume lags but still increases as price expands.

Source: © TradeStation Technologies, Inc. 1991–2005

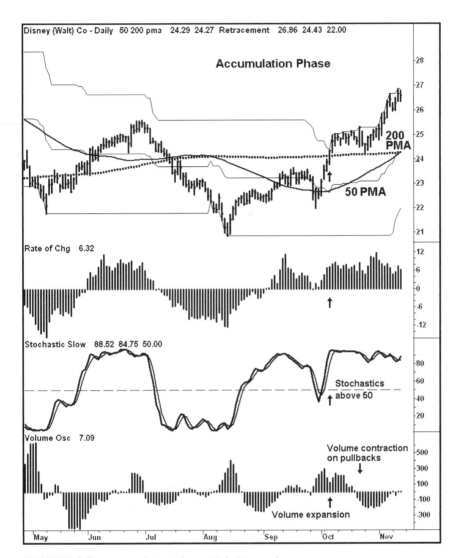

Disney (Walt) Co - Daily 50 200 pma 24.29 24.27 Retracement 26.86 24.43 22.00

Accumulation Phase

200 PMA

50 PMA

Rate of Chg 6.32

Stochastic Slow 88.52 84.75 50.00

Stochastics above 50

Volume Osc 7.09

Volume contraction on pullbacks

Volume expansion

FIGURE 4.5 Accumulation Phase: Walt Disney Company

The Accumulation Phase is often met with consolidation after the initial price expansion. The stochastics level in this phase is always above the 50 percent zone. After the consolidation, when price expands to new highs and closes high near the high, stochastics readings will shoot to very high levels. This is typical of an emerging uptrend—strong closes at new highs.

Source: © TradeStation Technologies, Inc. 1991–2005

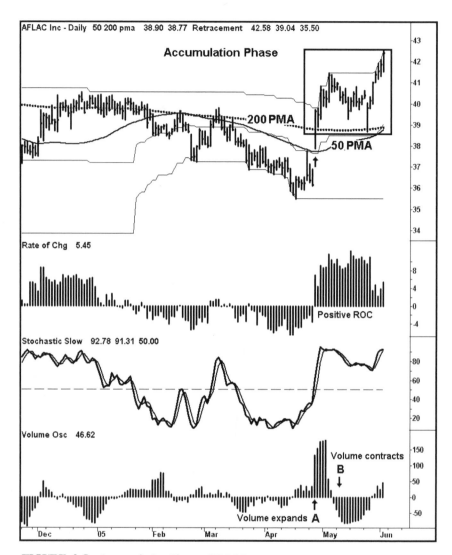

FIGURE 4.6 Accumulation Phase: AFLAC Inc.

After several months of fairly flat volume, price gaps into the Accumulation Phase on huge volume at point A. These price and volume expansion bars carried AFL into new 60 period price highs. Point B shows light volume on the pullback as price consolidates after the initial surge. Please note that volume is increasing again on the far right side of the chart as AFL is breaking out to more new highs.

Source: © TradeStation Technologies, Inc. 1991–2005

slower-to-respond 21 period moving average of volume (see Figure 4.6). After the price surges, there is likely to be price consolidation or a modest pullback. On this consolidation, one would want to see volume contract, which will cause the volume oscillator to go negative. The contraction in volume, combined with sideways price movement, means that buying has temporarily abated.

THE IDEAL ACCUMULATION PHASE CHARACTERISTICS

The best looking Accumulation Phase charts will have the following characteristics. If these conditions are present, the likelihood of positive phase progression is higher.

Buy Side	Accumulation Phase
50 PMA	Sloping up
200 PMA	Sideways with up bias
50% Retracement	Price above
60 period higher highs	Price making new 60 period higher highs
60 period higher lows	We begin to see 60 period higher lows
Rate of Change	In positive territory
Stochastic	Is above the 50 zone
Volume oscillator	Above zero on price expansion

The Ideal Accumulation Phase Chart

Figure 4.7 illustrates the components of the ideal Accumulation Phase chart.

The Weekly Accumulation Phase Chart

The *TREND*advisor Diamond Analysis works on different time frames, which makes it useful to a broad range of both traders and investors. For example, doing analysis on a weekly basis can be more appropriate for longer-term investors (like portfolio managers) who want to see the underlying trend. Longer time frames are what the biggest investing complexes that do technical analysis use. They do not want to respond to every blip in the market—their size makes it impossible to quickly get in or out of positions. This is why they use weekly charts—the longer time frame charts have less price volatility. Figure 4.8 shows an example of such weekly analysis.

The Ideal Accumulation Phase Chart

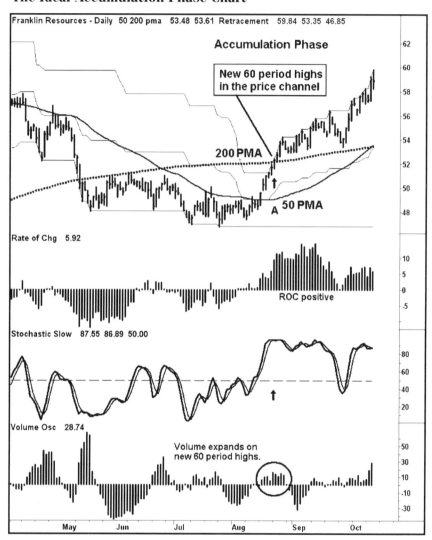

FIGURE 4.7 Accumulation Phase: Franklin Resources, Inc.
Components of the ideal Accumulation Phase chart are: at point A price moves into the Accumulation Phase after a long consolidation from May to August. With this close, the 50 PMA slope is now positive and the 200 PMA continues its upward slope. Price is breaking out to new 60 period highs. The 50 percent retracement of the 60 period high/low channel is now posting higher values as price expands. The momentum Rate of Change is clearly positive, and stochastics stay above the 50 zone except for minor pullback in the uptrend. Also, as price makes new 60 period highs, we see an expansion of volume. On pullbacks, there is a contraction in volume.
Source: © TradeStation Technologies, Inc. 1991–2005

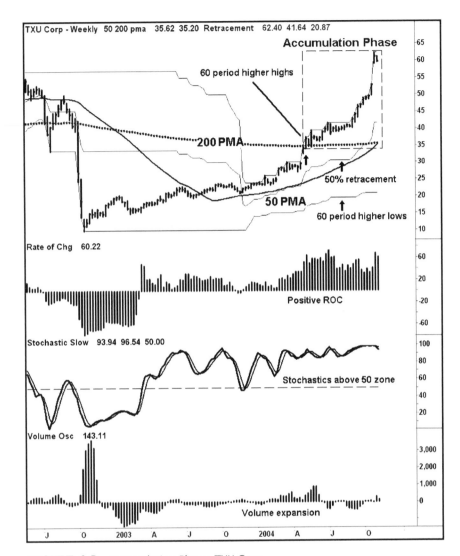

FIGURE 4.8 Accumulation Phase: TXU Corp.

The weekly chart of TXU exhibits all the characteristics necessary to see price expansion. We have price making new 60 period highs and new 60 period higher lows; the 200 PMA is flattening with a slight upward bias; the 50 PMA is sloping up; price holds above the 50 percent retracement area; the ROC is clearly positive; stochastics stay above the 50 zone; and the volume oscillator increases as price is making higher highs but contracts when price moves sideways.

Source: © TradeStation Technologies, Inc. 1991–2005

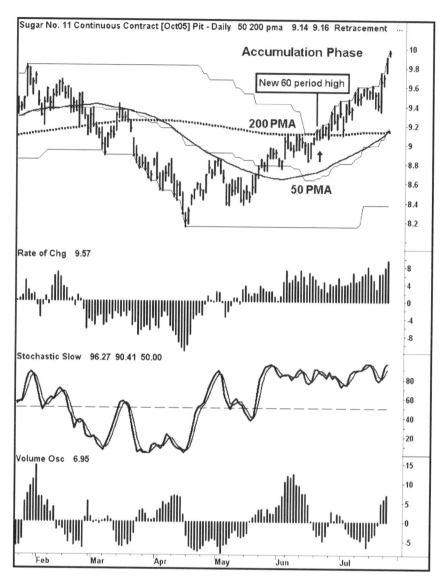

FIGURE 4.9 Accumulation Phase: Sugar

Sugar enters the Accumulation Phase when price crosses above the 200 PMA (see up arrow). This daily chart of sugar shows price then breaking into new 60 period highs. This is one of the positive characteristics of this chart along with the upward sloping 50 PMA. The continuation of positive ROC and stochastics above the 50 zone illustrates the ongoing buying interest where demand is increasing.
Source: © TradeStation Technologies, Inc. 1991–2005

Commodity: Daily Accumulation Phase Chart

The *TREND*advisor Diamond Analysis also works on different financial instruments. For example, the daily chart of sugar, shown in Figure 4.9, illustrates progression of the trend into the Accumulation Phase.

Mutual Fund: Weekly Accumulation Phase Chart

As we have seen in the preceding charts, The *TREND*advisor Diamond Analysis works on different instruments, which means both short term traders and long term investors can use it. Figure 4.10 shows the Accumulation Phase analysis as applied to a widely held mutual fund. Please note that there is no volume indictor for mutual funds because daily inflows and outflows change the amount in the pool of money in the fund. This is different from stocks and other financial instruments that have a fixed number of shares that change hands.

TRADING THE ACCUMULATION PHASE

When stocks enter the Accumulation Phase, the chances for further price increases get better. When the price first enters the Accumulation Phase by closing above the 200 PMA, price is now higher than the longer term trend. This is potentially significant, particularly if the slope of the 200 PMA is flat or slightly rising after a long basing period. The Accumulation Phase is the second phase on the buy side of the *TREND*advisor Diamond. It is a phase to consider when establishing additional long positions because trend is more in the investor's favor. The more trading criteria from the *TREND*advisor Diamond Matrix that the chart exhibits, the better the chances that a long trade may succeed (see the earlier Ideal Accumulation Phase Chart).

However, there is still risk when the Accumulation Phase begins because price has only recently exceeded the longer term trend. Also, when price first enters this phase, there still may be some time before we have a profit. These two factors mean we should use less capital than a full position.

Before we talk about guidelines for trading the Accumulation Phase, let's review some principles of capital allocation in a portfolio that we discussed in detail in Chapter 3. In short, be diversified across a number of positions because the fewer positions you have, the more concentrated you are, which usually means more risk. Professional money managers

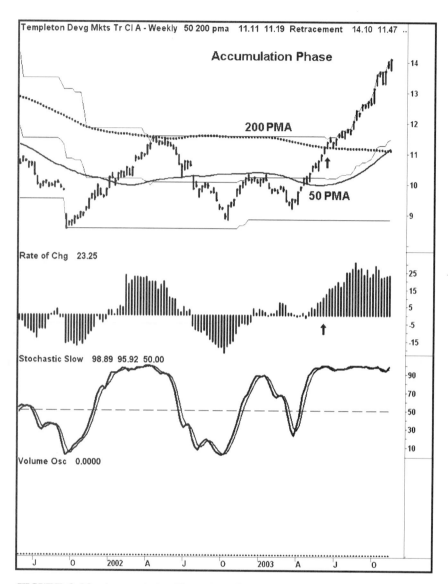

FIGURE 4.10 Accumulation Phase: Templeton Developing Markets Trust
The Templeton Developing Markets fund moves into the Accumulation Phase with
price closing above the 200 PMA (see up arrow). Price then penetrates the 60 period high channel. But look back earlier on the chart. At the beginning of 2002,
price made a move toward the Accumulation Phase but failed. That past price action was still digesting a steep decline in both the 50 and 200 PMA, whereas the
more recent Accumulation Phase price activity has had time to resolve the decline.
Source: © TradeStation Technologies, Inc. 1991–2005

are usually diversified across 10 or 20 positions at a minimum, and frequently more. Like the professional money managers, you also should be well diversified.

Trading tactics for this phase might include:

1. If you are going to establish new long positions in the Accumulation Phase, use two-thirds of the capital of what would be your usual, normal position size. This does two things. First, a smaller position size means you will have less capital at risk if the stock goes against you and you get stopped out. Second, you will have less capital tied up in something that may take time to produce profits.

2. *Always* have a stop. Your stop should be a logical place on the chart where the trade is clearly failing—for long positions, this could include a close below the 200 PMA, which would constitute a phase failure.

3. The longer the Accumulation Phase goes on, the more evidence you will have of how it is likely to resolve. If you look at Figures 4.2 through 4.7, you will see that after these stocks first entered the Accumulation Phase, even if they rallied initially, they consolidated before advancing again. Waiting for more evidence before entering a long in the Accumulation Phase makes sense. However, do recognize that in a strongly trending stock like the one shown in Figure 4.8, you will have to pay higher prices to get in and, if your stop is below the 200 PMA, your stop will be quite wide. As time goes on, more of the criteria for an ideal Accumulation Phase are met. Particularly, look for the 50 PMA sloping up. It is better if the 200 PMA is sideways, and best if it is sloping up. Price is above the 50 percent retracement line of the 60 period high/low channel. New 60 period highs should be occurring. The Rate of Change indicator is positive, stochastics are above the 50 zone and the volume oscillator is above zero, particularly on rallies, thus indicating a pickup in volume.

4. *Always* have a plan to capture profits. At *TREND*advisor, we harvest part of the trade when it hits the first profit target, and then raise our stop on the remaining portion to the entry price. By using this as our methodology, we book profits on part of our position. For the remaining part, we protect ourselves from a loss by setting the stop at breakeven, while allowing for additional profits if the stock continues to advance.

5. Take no short positions in this phase.

THE END OF THE ACCUMULATION PHASE

Part of our job as traders is to be vigilant to the end of trends that we are trading. The Accumulation Phase will end in one of two ways. It will either transition into the next positive phase or it will fail with a close back below the 50 PMA.

A transition into the next positive phase (the Bullish Phase) is covered in Chapter 5, and is the best outcome for an Accumulation Phase trade. However, as traders and investors, we have to be prepared that some of our trades will not work out. Our approach is to accept the reality that some things will not work and prepare you so you can identify what that looks like. Being prepared, knowing what to look for if something is not working will help you to act. Too many of the traders and investors we work with show up with no understanding of what to do when things go against them, and get paralyzed into inaction. This exacerbates losses. It is far better to realize, and be prepared, that some things will not work, and to look for the signs of an Accumulation Phase failure, and have in your trading plan the action steps you will take if it materializes.

ACCUMULATION PHASE FAILURE

It is not unusual for a stock to fail after it enters the Accumulation Phase for the first time. Figure 4.11 shows such a failure. If the price falls back below the 200 PMA, this means the phase has failed. An Accumulation Phase failure is more likely if the 200 PMA is sloping down (price is fighting the longer term trend) after a severe decline. Under those conditions, there is likely to be a significant spread between the 50 PMA and the 200 PMA, which would be additional evidence that the Phase may fail because there has not been enough time for the stock to heal after the substantial plummet. The ROC is small (indicating very little positive momentum). Stochastics may be above 50, indicating that closes are in the upper region of the recent range, but they start declining. If there is an absence of volume on the up move, it indicates not much buying interest in the stock even though the price has risen, and further confirms the chances for failure.

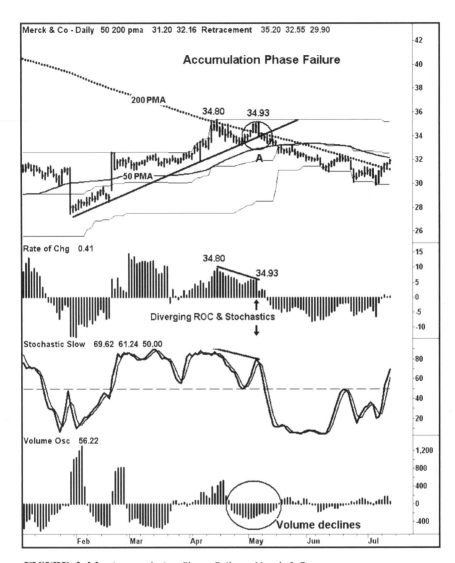

FIGURE 4.11 Accumulation Phase Failure: Merck & Co.
After deep declines, price begins to recover but often fails at a declining 200 PMA, point A. Additional clues are: diverging ROC and stochastics indicators. This is where price makes a new high (at point A), but the indicator makes a lower high than the preceding one (see downward sloping lines on the indicators). Also, the volume oscillator declining in the push up at point A is an additional clue to the failure. There was no volume, no demand, on that price increase.
Source: © TradeStation Technologies, Inc. 1991–2005

CHAPTER 5

The Bullish Phase

In Chapters 3 and 4, we have seen how prices evolve into the Recovery Phase and then progress into the Accumulation Phase. Next comes the Bullish Phase, where the uptrend is fully developing and further price increases are anticipated.

The Bullish Phase has the most positive characteristics of price activity, as shown in Figure 5.1. We liken it to going into the trading battle with a full team of soldiers behind you, yielding your best chance for success. In the Bullish Phase, the current close is greater than the 50 PMA and the 200 PMA, but most importantly, the 50 PMA is greater than the 200 PMA. With this precise definition in place, the analyst, trader, or investor can then further examine the quality of instruments in a Bullish Phase. The characteristics of the highest quality Bullish Phase are: first, a series of higher highs in the 60 period channel (coincident with an uptrend initiating or continuing), combined with, second, an upward sloping 50 PMA which, third, is above an upward sloping 200 PMA. Of these three, it is the continuing new highs in the 60 period high/low channel that confirm the uptrend as well as lead the 50 PMA and 200 PMA to continued increases.

TRADING DYNAMICS OF THE BULLISH PHASE

As the phases on the "buy side" of the *TREND*advisor Diamond progress, from Recovery to Accumulation to the Bullish Phase, we are getting

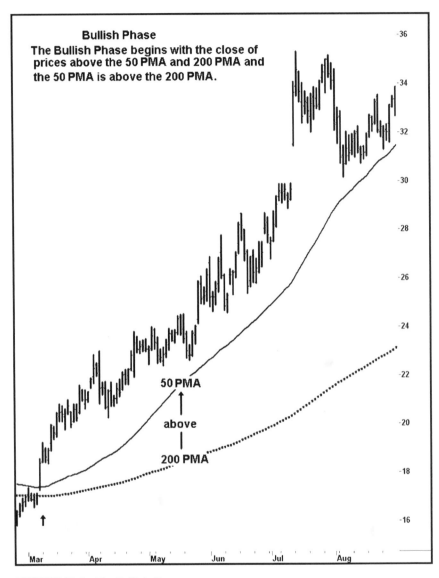

FIGURE 5.1   The Bullish Phase
Source: © TradeStation Technologies, Inc. 1991–2005

insights into the dynamics of the changing nature of the forces of supply and demand—the forces of buyers and sellers interacting.

In the Bullish Phase, intense buying (demand) is the dominant force in the dynamics of supply and demand. Please review the detailed discussion about these dynamics in Chapter 3. As a short summary: for every price that happens, there must be a buyer (creating demand) and a seller (creating supply). If there are buyers but no sellers, prices have to rise until sellers are induced to sell. If there are sellers but not buyers, then prices must fall until buyers are induced into buying.

In the Bullish Phase, with rising prices, one of several things must be happening. One possibility is that demand is staying the same, but supply is going down—if there are the same numbers of buyers for something, but supply drops, then prices will rise. If demand is increasing but supply stays the same, then price will rise as well.

- Prices rising can be caused by demand staying the same but supply decreasing.
- Prices rising can also be caused by demand increasing but supply staying the same.
- Prices rising can also be caused by demand rising faster than supply.
- If prices are going sideways, then demand and supply are in balance.

The Bullish Phase is evidence of demand far outstripping supply. In the Bullish Phase, what is generally going on is that buying pressure is so strong, and sellers are so sporadic, that prices are either rising sharply or consolidating at high levels after a rise.

Particularly in the early and midpart of the Bullish Phase demand is huge and there is little supply. With prices rallying, several things are happening.

Investors (the mutual fund portfolio managers and other professional investors) are completely convinced that they should own this instrument. If it is a stock, the conditions that are driving the earnings are so favorable that it is obvious to all the investors that this is a must-own name. Investors are not willing to sell—all the reasons that they took the risk and bought the stock are coming true—the new products are selling well, the economy is booming, management has effectively reduced costs or whatever the drivers are of the increasing earnings. The Bullish Phase shows complete confidence in the stock. There is an additional dynamic going on in the Bullish Phase with the professional investors. You may remember it from our discussion, in the Introduction, of the various players who show up in the market every day. In that discussion, we described how the mutual fund portfolio managers are paid on the performance of their portfolio relative to its benchmark index. We also described how many managers try to beat the benchmark index by underweighting, or not owning, the stocks they think will not be good performers. If a stock is underweighted in their portfolio, and it starts to rally strongly, the benchmark index will start to outperform the portfolio manager's fund. This forces the manager into buying the stock—if he doesn't get it into his portfolio, the benchmark index will continue to outperform, and he will lose his bonus or his job. This dynamic of having to own a name that is outperforming helps to fuel rallies in the Bullish Phase. If the investment is a commodity, there is a change in the underlying dynamics of demand (China as the world's largest developing economy is consuming much more oil); or something is happening that causes a sharp drop in supply (a freeze in Florida kills the orange crop).

As prices rally, a second factor kicks in. Remember our discussion about the professional short sellers, who make money when the market is declining? In a strong rally, if they try to short, they have losers. One of the dynamics in the Bullish Phase is that there are very few traders willing to short into the rally. They don't want to short while prices are rising, because those shorts lose money as prices go up. The traders and managers of hedge funds, who get paid on absolute performance, do not want losers because their paychecks will get cut.

Additionally, with prices rallying, the sophisticated traders, those in the markets every day, increase their buying. The more prices rally, creating an uptrend, the more likely there will be traders buying breakouts at new highs and also buying the dips. These traders are much less likely to be selling rallies, which would constrain price, at least early on in the Bullish Phase. They are much more likely to be buying, creating underlying demand.

However, as the Bullish Phase matures, one of the things to look for is a willingness of traders to start to sell at resistance, to sell where sellers have shown up before. We will look at this in more detail later in the chapter.

In short, in the Bullish Phase, buying pressure is high. Equally important, there are very few sellers. As you can see, there are several groups who are competing in purchasing and very few willing to sell—this is what causes prices to rise sharply, particularly early in the phase.

IDENTIFYING POTENTIAL TRADING CANDIDATES IN THE BULLISH PHASE

There are several characteristics that financial instruments will exhibit if they are potential Bullish Phase trading candidates. Instruments that do not meet these criteria do not qualify to be potential candidates. We are training your eye to see what good potential candidates look like.

In the Bullish Phase, the 60 period low channel indicator is frequently rising, indicating that price lows have been stepping up for some time. This is telling us that lows are rising. The 60 period high channel indicator is frequently rising, meaning there are new price highs. Because an uptrend is defined as a series of higher highs with higher lows in between, new highs in the 60 period channel is the best evidence of the uptrend extending.

The Bullish Phase is when prices are trending sharply up over time. The Bullish Phase is characterized by:

- A series of higher price highs and higher price lows
- Upward sloping 50 and 200 period moving averages
- Powerful momentum (larger price moves in short time frames), which will display as large, positive readings in the ROC and stochastics indicators
- Stochastics above the 50 zone
- Accelerating volume

Look for the following characteristics in our indicators in the Bullish Phase to identify potential trading candidates.

60 Period High/Low Channel

The first guides we use to identify the Bullish Phase are *higher highs*, as shown in Figure 5.2. We identify higher highs by creating a line that shows the value of what the highest high has been for the last 60 periods. (We use 60 periods because it's a close approximation of a quarter of the year.) We then can see where the current price is relative to whatever the highest high has been for the previous 60 periods. When prices start to exceed this line, we can state that the market is now producing the higher highs that define an uptrend.

50 and 200 Period Moving Average

In the Bullish Phase, the close is above both the 50 and the 200 period moving averages and the 50 PMA is above the 200 PMA. The phase can begin in one of two ways. Price can cross above the 50 PMA with it being above the 200 PMA (see Figures 5.4 to 5.9 as examples). Also, it is not unusual for the Bullish Phase to begin by the 50 PMA crossing above the 200 PMA as its trigger (see Figures 5.3 and 5.10 as examples). The 50 PMA

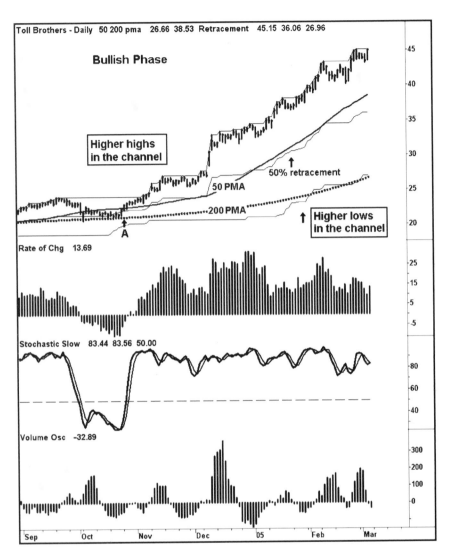

FIGURE 5.2 Bullish Phase: Toll Brothers

At point A price crosses above the 50 PMA and the 50 PMA is above the 200 PMA, putting TOL into the Bullish Phase. With the 60 period high/low channel making higher highs and higher lows (see text boxes on chart), this results in a rising 50 percent retracement level. The rising 50 and 200 PMAs show the uptrend strengthening as prices continue to expand.

Source: © TradeStation Technologies, Inc. 1991–2005

should be rising—a rising PMA means that the recent trend has turned upward. If the 200 PMA is flat or rising slightly, this means that price has been going sideways, on average, for some time, which indicates a long basing pattern. Higher prices will quickly kick that average positive. Frequently, also, the 200 PMA will be flattening out, signifying that the longer term price action has been moving sideways for some time. In a Bullish Phase that represents a long basing pattern, the 50 PMA and the 200 PMA will be converging.

Why use a 200 period moving average? Our job as traders is to identify trends and effectively trade them because trading with trend provides us the quickest, biggest profit in the shortest period. Usually, trends do not end quickly nor do they end with a sharp, substantial reversal in price. Therefore, a longer moving average can better help us to see the longer trend of prices, which can better help us to be trading with that trend.

Conditions for an emerging uptrend include: a series of higher highs, prices closing above a 50 period moving average and the 200 period moving average, and the 200 period moving average is moving up.

What this congregation is telling us is that prices are moving up (the higher highs), and that the current price is above two averages of recent price. The 50 period moving average being above the 200 period moving average is telling us that more recent prices have, on average, been above longer term price averages. The upward sloping moving average tells us that, on average, prices have been increasing sufficiently to pull the average of prices up.

If the 50 period moving average is close to the 200 period moving average and the price is slightly above both, this is telling us that the price has been "clustering" for some time, meaning that current price is very close but above recent price, and recent price averages are very close to a longer term average of prices—prices are very much the same over time. Once prices break out above this clustering phase, this starts an emerging uptrend. Mathematically, you can see why—the higher prices are trend, and those higher prices will pull the averages up behind them.

If you think about this in terms of supply and demand, the clustering of price, short term and longer term moving averages, represents equilibrium of supply and demand—nothing is moving much over time. When prices start up from a condition of equilibrium, which usually means demand is outstripping supply—this is a precursor to more significant price action. As you will read shortly, we can get excellent confirmation if demand is increasing by analyzing volume.

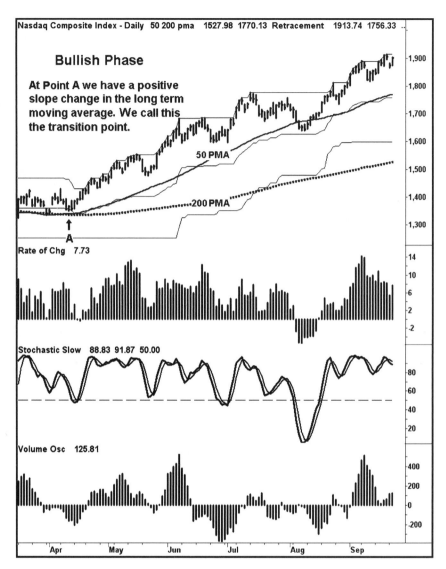

FIGURE 5.3   Bullish Phase: NASDAQ Composite Index
The NASDAQ Index enters the Bullish Phase at point A where the 50 PMA crosses above the 200 PMA. Note that price is already above the 50 PMA, so when the 50 crosses above the 200, that triggers the Bullish Phase starting. Also, at point A the slope of the 200 PMA moves from down to up. We call this the transition point. When this occurs in the Bullish Phase and is coupled with the upward sloping 50 PMA, the likelihood of further price gains often exists.
Source: © TradeStation Technologies, Inc. 1991–2005

Upward Sloping Moving Averages and Transition Point

In the Bullish Phase, a high quality uptrend will have both an upward sloping 50 and upward sloping 200. The transition point is when the 200 period moving average moves from going down to starting up; in other words, this period's 200 PMA is greater than last period's 200 PMA. This is telling us that the longer term trend has changed from down to up, or that the slope of the longer term trend has transitioned to up. (See Figure 5.3.)

Rate of Change Indicator

In the Bullish Phase, the trend is up. This means that prices will be consistently above where they were 21 periods ago, so the Rate of Change indicator will be positive, as in Figure 5.4. If it pulls back to zero (or goes slightly negative), this is showing periods of consolidation that frequently happen after price surges.

Stochastics

In an uptrend, there will be higher highs. Please remember that stochastics are measuring close relative to recent range. This means that in the Bullish Phase, the range calculation part of stochastics will be increasing, as shown in Figure 5.5. In uptrends, prices close high in the range. Therefore, stochastics readings will be persistently high.

Volume Oscillator

If higher prices are occurring and volume is increasing, this can only mean that demand is outstripping supply—there are more transactions happening even as prices advance. Volume surges on rallies are confirming the underlying dynamics of demand for the stock. This means the volume oscillator will rise on price rallies, as shown in Figure 5.6. It should decrease when prices consolidate after the surges, which indicates abatement in buying.

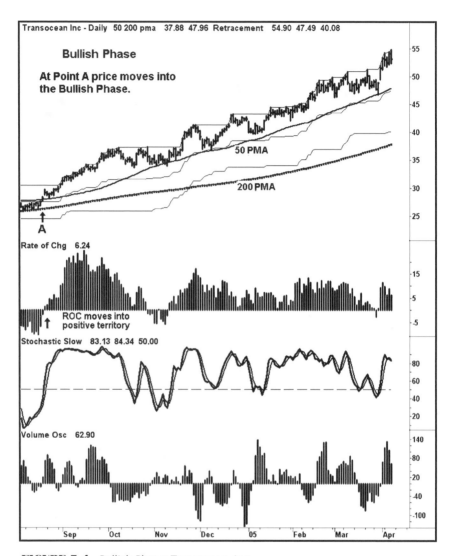

FIGURE 5.4 Bullish Phase: Transocean, Inc.

The Bullish Phase begins as price crosses above the 50 PMA and the 50 PMA is greater than the 200 PMA (see the up arrow). At point A, with price moving into the Bullish Phase, the ROC (momentum) turns positive. Next, price expands, making higher highs and higher lows, which show up in the 60 period channel as a series of rising steps.

Source: © TradeStation Technologies, Inc. 1991–2005

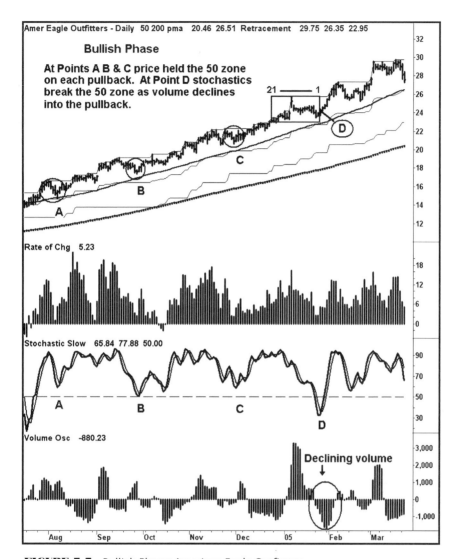

FIGURE 5.5 Bullish Phase: American Eagle Outfitters
With stochastics measuring the current close in relationship to its recent range, in a strong uptrend stochastics level will stay above the 50 zone. Note that in a strong uptrend pullbacks to the upward sloping 50 PMA and pullbacks in stochastics to the 50 zone can be excellent buying opportunities (see the Trading section). This happens at points A, B and C. At point D, the close in relation to its range over the 21 periods has a value of 35. This lower reading in stochastics is an example of what could be an excellent buying opportunity, if all the other conditions are in place.
Source: © TradeStation Technologies, Inc. 1991–2005

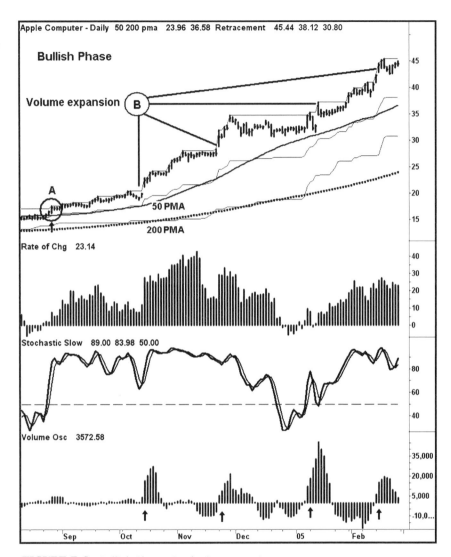

FIGURE 5.6 Bullish Phase: Apple Computer, Inc.

At point A, price closes above the 50 PMA, placing AAPL in the Bullish Phase because the 50 PMA is already above the 200 PMA. There is excellent volume expansion as price gaps into new 60 period highs (see the four examples radiating from B with the corresponding up arrows on the volume oscillator) with upward sloping 50 and 200 PMAs. These volume and price expansion moves are common to the Bullish Phase as all components of trend are in place.

Source: © TradeStation Technologies, Inc. 1991–2005

THE IDEAL BULLISH PHASE CHARACTERISTICS

The best looking Bullish Phase charts will have the following characteristics. If these conditions are present, the likelihood of positive phase progression is higher.

Buy Side	Bullish Phase
50 PMA	Sloping up
200 PMA	Sloping up
50% Retracement	Price above
60 period higher highs	Price making new 60 period higher highs
60 period higher lows	Channel making 60 period higher lows
Rate of Change	In positive territory
Stochastic	Is above the 50 zone
Volume oscillator	Above zero on price expansion

The Ideal Bullish Phase Chart

See Figure 5.7 on the following page.

Weekly Bullish Phase Chart

The weekly chart in Figure 5.8 is an example of the strength of the Bullish Phase.

Commodity: Weekly Bullish Phase Chart

The *TREND*advisor Diamond Analysis also works on different financial instruments. For example, the weekly chart of Crude Oil shows progression of the trend into the Bullish Phase (see Figure 5.9). Note that once the uptrend was clearly established, each pullback in the phase met with buyers. This is showing the dynamics of how the professional traders trade the trend—as long as it is intact, they buy the pullbacks as well as the breakouts.

Mutual Fund: Weekly Bullish Phase Chart

The preceding chart (Figure 5.9) showed a commodity, Crude Oil. Many investors do not trade commodities. However, because the *TREND*advisor Diamond Analysis works on different instruments and can be used by both investors and traders, a mutual fund investor could similarly profit from the long term trend in Crude as the commodities trader in the previous chart does. Figure 5.10 shows the Bullish Phase analysis as applied to a widely held energy mutual fund.

The Ideal Bullish Phase Chart

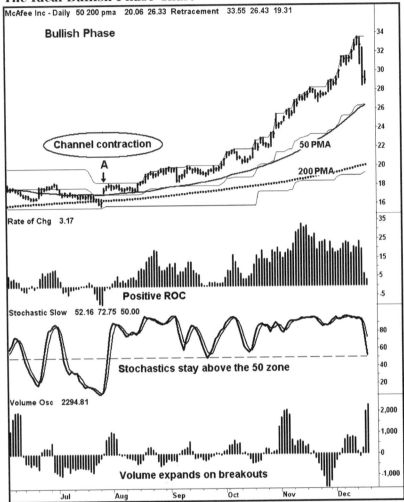

FIGURE 5.7 Bullish Phase: McAfee, Inc.

Components of the ideal Bullish Phase chart include: at point A price crosses above the 50 PMA, placing MFE in the Bullish Phase (the 50 PMA is already above the 200 PMA). With this positive close, the 50 PMA slope is positive along with the 200 PMA (transition point). Note that the moving averages are quite close to each other, illustrating that a long period of consolidation has happened. Price is also closing above the 50 percent retracement level of the contracting 60 period high/low channel. The momentum Rate of Change becomes clearly positive, and stochastics stay above the 50 zone. Also, as price makes new 60 period highs, there is an expansion of volume; on pullbacks there is a contraction in volume. These higher highs are what pull the averages up, kicking in the uptrend.

Source: © TradeStation Technologies, Inc. 1991–2005

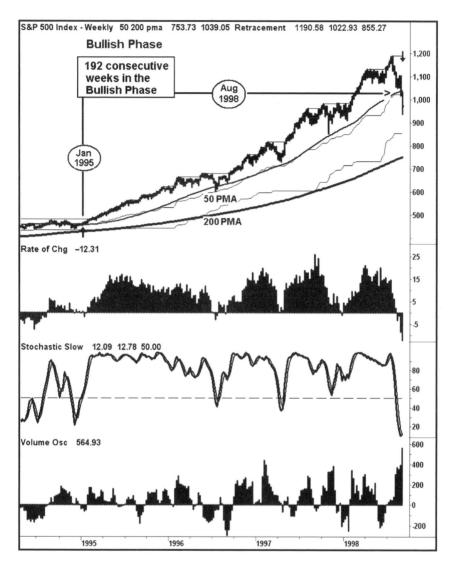

FIGURE 5.8 Bullish Phase: S&P 500 Index

The weekly chart of the S&P 500 is a great example of the strength of the Bullish Phase on a long term trend chart. In January 1995 price crossed above the 50 PMA, placing the S&P 500 in the Bullish Phase. Over the span of 192 consecutive weeks, the S&P 500 stayed in the Bullish Phase. On several occasions price tested the 50 PMA but never closed below it until August 1998.

Source: © TradeStation Technologies, Inc. 1991–2005

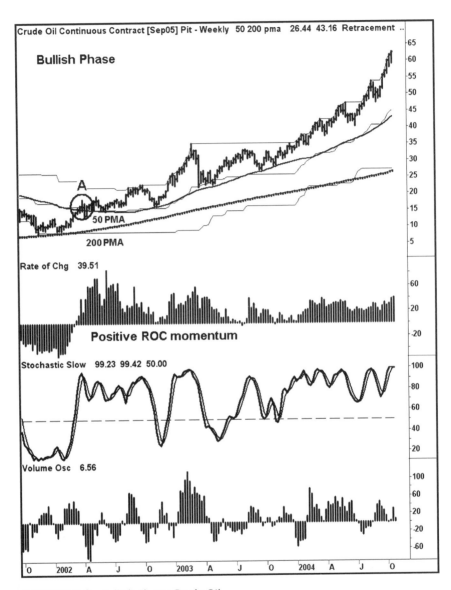

FIGURE 5.9 Bullish Phase: Crude Oil
The Bullish Phase chart of Crude Oil demonstrates the strength of this phase. At point A price moves into the phase with all indicators in sync. As price begins to expand we see the frequency of new 60 period highs. This price expansion creates a steeper incline to the slope of both the 50 and 200 PMA, keeping the ROC positive for several years.
Source: © TradeStation Technologies, Inc. 1991–2005

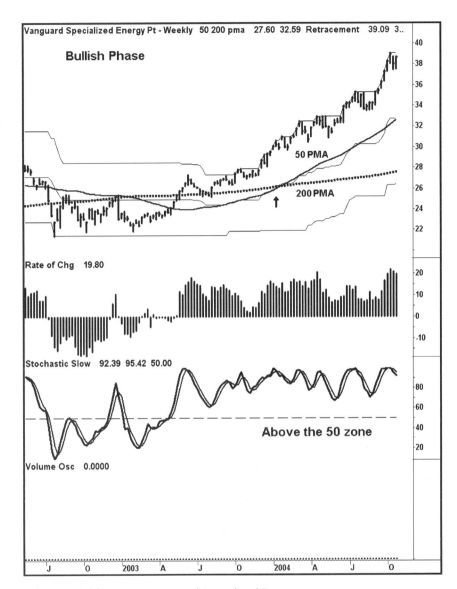

FIGURE 5.10 Bullish: Vanguard Specialized Energy
This chart has the Bullish Phase starting with the 50 PMA crossing above the 200 PMA (see up arrow). In this example price is already above the 50 PMA, so it is the moving average crossing above that triggers the phase. This type of price action often could be very powerful because the 50 PMA lagged the 200 PMA, suggesting time was needed to build a base. When that base was resolved, note that price broke out into new 60 period highs, establishing the uptrend. Stochastic stays above the 50 zone for an extended period of time, indicating high closes, which are typical of a long established uptrend.
Source: © TradeStation Technologies, Inc. 1991–2005

TRADING THE BULLISH PHASE

When stocks enter the Bullish Phase, the chances for further price increases get better. When the Bullish Phase begins with price being above the 50 PMA and 200 PMA and the 50 PMA is above the 200 PMA, current trend is up, recent trend (as evidenced by the 50 PMA) is above long term trend (as evidenced by the 200 PMA). This is potentially significant because it indicates the potential for further, powerful up moves. The Bullish Phase is the third phase on the "buy side" of the *TREND*advisor Diamond. It is a phase to consider when establishing additional long positions because trend is in our favor. The more trading criteria from the *TREND*advisor Diamond Matrix that the chart exhibits, the better the chances a long trade may succeed (see the earlier Ideal Bullish Phase Chart).

As the Bullish Phase begins, particularly if the ideal criteria are met, the chances for success are very good. Therefore, this is a phase for considering using a full capital position.

Before we talk about guidelines for trading the Bullish Phase, let's review some principles of capital allocation in a portfolio that we discussed in Chapter 3. In short, be diversified across a number of positions because the fewer positions you have, the more concentrated you are, which usually means more risk. Professional money managers are usually diversified across 10 or 20 positions at a minimum, and frequently more. Like the professional money managers, you also should be well diversified.

Trading tactics for this phase might include:

1. If you are going to establish new long positions in the Bullish Phase, consider a full, normal position size.

2. *Always* have a stop. Your stop should be a logical place on the chart where the trade is clearly failing. For long positions, this could include a close below the 50 PMA, which would constitute a phase failure.

3. The longer the Bullish Phase goes on, the more evidence you will have of how it is resolving. It may be better to enter your position early in the phase as long as the criteria for an ideal Bullish Phase are met. Early entry means you will have profits as the phase progresses, if price continues to trend up. In order to enter, look for the 50 PMA to be sloping up. Additionally, the 200 PMA should be sloping up. Price is above the 50 percent retracement line of the 60 period high/low channel, the 50 percent retracement line must be

rising, and there should be new 60 period highs and higher 60 period lows. The Rate of Change indicator is positive, stochastics are persistently above the 50 zone, and frequently quite high. In the Bullish Phase, the volume oscillator very often declines on consolidations, indicating light volume on pullbacks. It should move above zero on rallies to indicate a pickup in volume. Late in the Bullish Phase, a sign of its potentially tiring is that there is no surge of volume on the rallies.

4. *Always* have a plan to capture profits. At *TREND*advisor, we harvest part of the trade when it hits the first profit target, and then raise our stop on the remaining portion to the entry price. By using this as our methodology, we book profits on part of our position. For the remaining part, we protect ourselves from a loss by setting the stop at breakeven, while allowing for additional profits if the stock continues to advance.

5. Take no short positions in this phase.

There are a variety of ways to trade the Bullish Phase but we will focus on two: buying the breakouts (buying strength), or buying the consolidations (buying weakness in underlying strength). The conditions and rules described below are based on daily chart analysis.

At *TREND*advisor, our focus is on shorter term trading—our positions are on for only a matter of days. Given that this is our objective, the *TREND*advisor Diamond Trading Methodology is based on:

- Opportunities that can produce 3 percent to 7 percent on any one trade based on our plan. For longer term investors, clearly the objective will be higher.
- Stop orders to exit and enter at points specified by the methodology.

Each trade complies with specified rules in the Plan Objectives and Plan Strategy, and reflects sound money management. The Bullish Phase is the most popular and exciting phase of stock investing. This phase is often the start of a major trend. Some of its characteristics are:

- Prices rise rapidly.
- Volume increases along with price.
- Buyers become aggressive and buy on strength as well as on weakness.
- Breakaway price gaps occur often, usually on heavier volume.

Bullish Phase Conditions

- Price closes are above the 50 period moving average.
- Price closes are above the 200 period moving average.
- 50 period moving average is above the 200 period moving average.

Purchasing financial instruments when their price structure meets the above criteria often leads to safe opportunities over all time frames. However, for long-term buy and hold strategies where the security is to be held for months or years, this timing method will insure strategic entries and greater rewards based on a sound trading plan.

The criteria for buying strength in the Bullish Phase are:

- Price is breaking out to new 60 period highs.
- The 50 and 200 moving averages are sloping up, or the last period is greater than the previous period.
- The Rate of Change indicator is above the zero line and accelerating to the upside (this tells us we have positive momentum).
- The stochastics indicator is above the 50 zone and rising (this tells us we are closing in the upper 50 percent of our defined range).
- Volume is increasing as our volume oscillator moves above the zero line (this tells us our short term moving average of volume is expanding above the longer term moving average).

Rules to Entry

Screen stocks that meet the above criteria.

To open a position on the *long side: buy* when the stock price trades 1/8 to 3/8 above yesterday's high (the 1/8 to 3/8 range should be based on price and volatility of the stock).

Rules to Exits

Initial *stop*: Your stop should be a logical place on the chart where the trade is clearly failing. For long positions, this could include a close below the 50 PMA, which would constitute a phase failure.

Always harvest profits: Sell half of the position at a target price objective, based on your trading plan, then manage the remaining half of the position. As price moves higher, place a trailing stop at the entry price and let the price move continue up (or down) until the price stops at the last target.

Sell at less than target when price (volume) stalls (see Bullish Phase failure).

Sell remaining position when the phase changes.

RULES TO TRADE

Trade with the Market

Stock candidates should be chosen based on the individual's plan objective and risk tolerance. Trading with the market allows the investor or trader the benefit of market momentum. For instance, you might buy Intel because it provided you with the appropriate entry opportunity. (This issue is also traded in the baskets of NASDAQ 100, S&P 100, S&P 500, Dow Jones Industrials, Semiconductor Index, and ETFs.) Having the benefit of the market momentum and the basket purchases behind you on an issue like INTC, the opportunity for price expansion is greatly increased. Candidates with high deltas in a Bullish Phase also increase your winning percentages (high delta or high beta means that an individual stock outperforms the market).

Trade with the Sectors

We use the acronym MSE, meaning trade in the direction of the Market first, followed by the Sector, and then use a top-down approach to those Equities meeting your criteria. The market is the engine that pulls along the sectors and the equities. When we have all this in sync the likelihood of trading success is greatly enhanced.

Buying Pullbacks

In the Bullish Phase, prices often retreat to the upward sloping 50 period moving average, offering an excellent buying opportunity. Prices will also retreat to a 50 percent retracement of the 60 period high/low channels. Volume is very often likely to be lighter on these pullbacks because buyers are unwilling to give up the price of the security at the lower levels, suggesting strength. Entries in the Bullish Phase should be timed with the overall market and accompanying industry sector. Therefore, if the market and industry sectors are rising and in the Bullish Phase, look for stocks that also are in the Bullish Phase. Taking it one step further, the investors and traders who purchased in the Recovery Phase are probably looking to harvest a portion of their profits but not willing to give up the full position. This is why volume is often lighter on these pullbacks, yet the overall trend is still intact.

CONDITIONS TO BUY IN BULLISH PHASE

- Price breaking above a rising 50 PMA.
- Price rebounds off the 50 percent retracement level of the 60 period high/low channel.
- Price breaks out to new 60 period high.
- The Rate of Change indicator moves up through the zero line, suggesting a rise in momentum.
- Stochastics move above the 50 zone, telling us the close is in the upper 50 percent of the range.
- Volume oscillator breaks above the zero line; this supports near term buying interest.

Bear Fake Buying Opportunity

The Bear Fake is a bullish buying opportunity. The setup unfolds by first scouting for a price close below an upward sloping 50 PMA; price is above the upward sloping 200 PMA and the 50 PMA is above the 200 PMA. (See Figures 5.11 through 5.13.) This alerts us to a potential Bear Fake buying opportunity. Once the above conditions have been met, we then watch for price to close above the upward sloping 50 PMA, usually within one to six periods. This triggers the buy, and a long position is then established. What actually takes place is price reverses from the Bullish Phase to the Warning Phase, and then reverts back into the Bullish Phase, usually within one to six periods; this is nothing more than a pullback in an uptrend.

Characteristics of Bear Fake Setups

- Upward sloping 50 and 200 PMA.
- Higher highs and higher lows in the 60 period high/low channel.
- Price above the 50 percent retracement level of the 60 period high/low channel.
- The Rate of Change indicator above the zero line suggests a rise in momentum.
- Stochastics above the 50 zone tells us the close is in the upper 50 percent of the range.
- Volume oscillator above the zero line supports near term buying interest.
- Entries should be timed with a rising market and rising sector.

NASDAQ—Bear Fake Strategy

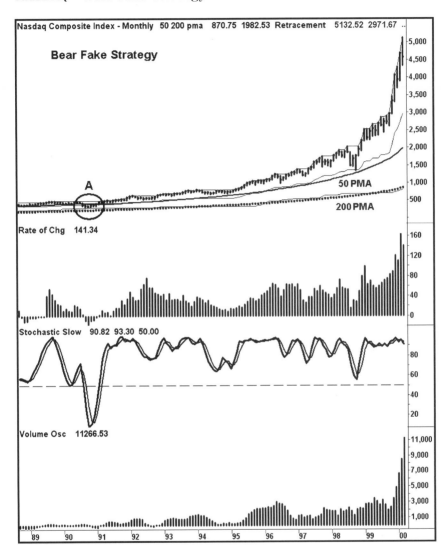

FIGURE 5.11 Bear Fake Strategy: NASDAQ Composite Index

The Bear Fake strategy is a very compelling setup when all characteristics are in place. First we scout for price moving below an upward sloping 50 PMA with an upward sloping 200 PMA, as seen at point A. The key to this setup is having price stay below the 50 PMA for one to six periods. We then watch for price closing above the 50 PMA while taking out the prior bar high. This strategy is nothing more than a short term pullback in an uptrend.

Source: © TradeStation Technologies, Inc. 1991–2005

Soybeans—Bear Fake Strategy

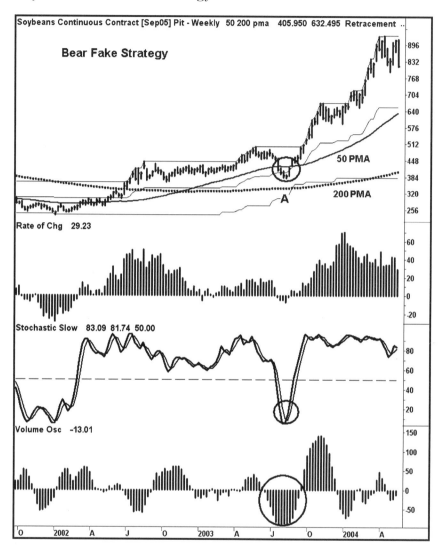

FIGURE 5.12   Bear Fake Strategy: Soybeans

The Bear Fake strategy on the soybean weekly chart displays the pullback after an expansion trend. At point A price moves below the upward sloping 50 PMA and upward sloping 200 PMA. Once price closes above the 50 PMA within one to six periods and the high is greater than the high of the prior bar, the strategy is confirmed. Here we had stochastic at the lower end of its recent range, with the volume oscillator suggesting the absence of selling pressure.

Source: © TradeStation Technologies, Inc. 1991–2005

CFC—Bear Fake Strategy

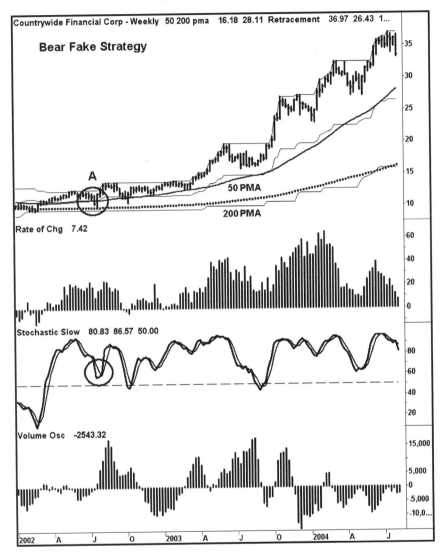

FIGURE 5.13 Bear Fake Strategy: Countrywide Financial Corp.
The Bear Fake strategy on the weekly CFC chart meets all the criteria of this powerful setup. At point A price moves below the upward sloping 50 PMA with a rising 200 PMA. This setup pullback was only one bar below the 50 PMA, suggesting the lack of selling pressure. This is also seen by the ROC momentum on the plus side and stochastic value in the upper 60 percent of its recent range.
Source: © TradeStation Technologies, Inc. 1991–2005

THE END OF THE BULLISH PHASE

Part of our job as traders is to be vigilant to the end of trends that we are trading. The end of the Bullish Phase is characterized by several events, the first of which is the absence of new price highs being made over time. This is coupled with a flat-lined 60 period high channel indicator.

As traders and investors, we have to realize that some of our trades will not work out. Our approach is to accept the reality that some things will not work and prepare you so you can identify what that looks like. Being prepared, knowing what to look for if something is not working, will help you to act. Too many of the traders and investors we work with show up with no understanding of what to do when things go against them, and get paralyzed into inaction. This exacerbates losses. It is far better to realize, and be prepared, that some things will not work, and to look for signs of a Bullish Phase failure, and have in your trading plan the action steps you will take if it materializes.

In a maturing Bullish Phase, particularly after a long uptrend, as time progresses price begins to move sideways, often with a slight downward bias. If this is the case, the moving averages are going to catch up to price—either because price drops to them or the averages rise to price. As this begins to unfold, prices will start to close below the upward sloping 50 moving average. The market begins to lose the strong momentum that the characterizes Bullish Phase and our two momentum indicators will start to exhibit signs of weakness.

Our Rate of Change indicator will not be rising sharply the way it was when prices originally surged. And our stochastics will start giving us low readings, telling us that current and recent closes are at the lower end of the recent range. In an uptrending market, the first closes below the 50 period moving average may only signify pullbacks to the upward sloping 50 moving average. If prices quickly rebound, and start closing back above the moving average, these short periods of tests of the 50 period moving average are Bear Fakes and are tradable. Time is frequently a factor in the failure of a Bullish Phase. This can materialize in several ways. One of these is that the highest high channel starts to decline, signifying lower highs are materializing. Another can be that the lower channel starts to decline, signifying lower lows are appearing. As time marches on, price will start to consistently and consecutively close below the 50 period moving average, and that 50 period moving average will start pointing down. This leads us to the conditions for the Warning Phase, which we will examine in Chapter 6.

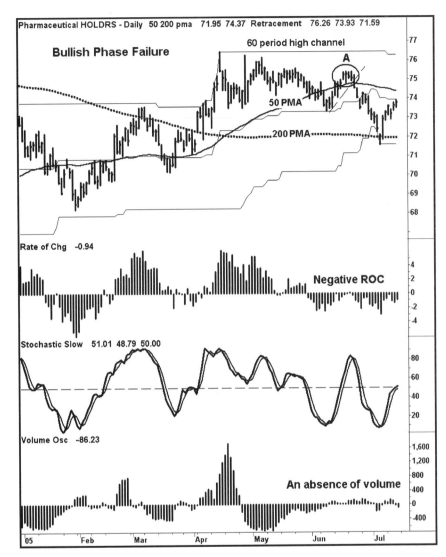

FIGURE 5.14 Bullish Phase Failure: Pharmaceutical Holders

At point A price moves up into the Bullish Phase, but we have a flat 50 PMA and a flattening 200 PMA. There have been no new highs in the 60 period high/low channel for months, indicating no further uptrend. The ROC momentum has not participated in this most recent advance and we see an absence of volume. These classic signs provide us with clues to what to look for in this failure pattern.

Source: © TradeStation Technologies, Inc. 1991–2005

BULLISH PHASE FAILURE

Bullish Phase failures are often a function of a tired, extensive topping process after an uptrend as shown in Figure 5.14 on previous page. Price has been moving sideways, not making new 60 period highs. If the price falls back below the 50 PMA, this means the phase has failed. Buying pressure has subsided, suggesting that traders are unwilling to bid up the price. A Bullish Phase failure is more likely if the 200 PMA is flat or beginning to slope down, indicating that the long uptrend has lost its power, similar to being in the ninth inning of a nine-inning game. Under those conditions, there is likely to be little spread between the 50 PMA and the 200 PMA, which would be additional evidence that the phase may fail. The ROC may be negative, indicating an inability for price to be above the preceding highs. Stochastic may be above 50, indicating that closes are in the upper region of the recent range, but it starts declining. If there is an absence of volume, the 5 period moving average of volume will either be below the 21 period moving average of volume or weakly wafting above and below it. This will cause the volume oscillator to be flat or negative.

CHAPTER 6

The Warning Phase

The Warning Phase is when investors have accumulated as much stock as they can consume and prices begin to plateau (Figure 6.1). Traders start taking their profits. This phase marks the start of what may be the topping pattern, signaling that investors are not only no longer aggressively buying the stock, but they are now beginning to take profits. What frequently precedes the Warning Phase is a long period of flattening price action. The Warning Phase begins when prices start to close below the 50 PMA.

The Warning Phase is similar to the top of the bell curve. We now have our current close less than the 50 PMA, but we still have a positive close greater than the 200 PMA, and the relationship of the 50 PMA is greater than the 200 PMA. In this price configuration, current price is weaker than recent prices but the price structure historically has been relatively strong. Price below a downward sloping 50 PMA is a more severe warning than if the 50 PMA is still upward. With an uptrend defined as a series of higher highs with higher lows in between, the absence of new highs in the 60 period channel is the best evidence of the uptrend ending.

TRADING DYNAMICS OF THE WARNING PHASE

The Warning Phase is the first phase on the "sell side" of the *TREND*advisor Diamond. The dynamics of the changing nature of the forces of supply and demand—the forces of buyers and sellers interacting—is what we see

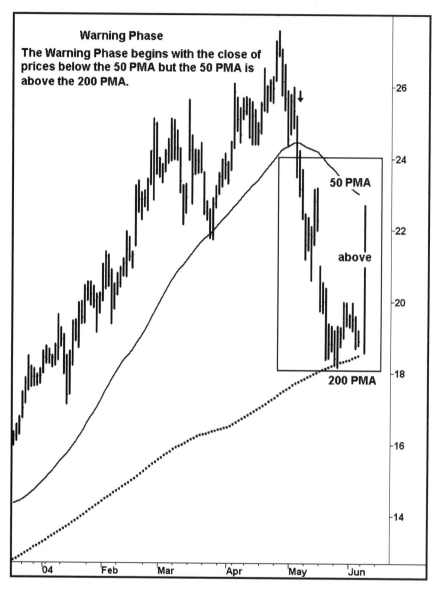

Warning Phase

The Warning Phase begins with the close of
prices below the 50 PMA but the 50 PMA is
above the 200 PMA.

FIGURE 6.1   The Warning Phase
Source: © TradeStation Technologies, Inc. 1991–2005

as the phases progress. In the Warning Phase, what is generally going on is that buying pressure is drying up—there are no more buyers to buy.

Please review the detailed discussion about these dynamics in Chapter 3. As a short summary: for every price that happens, there must be a buyer (creating demand) and a seller (creating supply). If there are sellers but no buyers, then prices must fall until buyers are induced into buying. If there are buyers but not sellers, prices have to rise until sellers are induced to sell.

In the Warning Phase, if prices are falling, one of several things must be happening. One possibility is that supply is staying the same, but demand is going down—if there are the same numbers of sellers for something, but buyers stop buying (demand drops), then prices will fall. If supply is increasing, but demand stays the same, then prices will fall.

- Prices falling can be caused by supply staying the same but demand decreasing.
- Prices falling can be caused by supply increasing but demand staying the same.
- Prices falling can be caused by supply rising faster than demand.
- If prices are going sideways, then supply and demand are in balance.

In the Warning Phase, buying pressure is usually drying up. This means that demand has fallen. While prices were going up, there were plenty of buyers willing to jump into the market. These buyers included both those who wanted to be long because of the increases in prices, and the short sellers, if any, who were losing money on the rallies and had to cover. However, as prices start to flatten out, several things start happening.

The professional investors, such as mutual fund managers, make their decisions based on the forecast of what they calculate a company will earn, and what the future discounted value of those earnings will be. If the stock price is selling well above the calculated value, the investor has to either increase the target value or sell the stock because it is too expensive relative to what it will earn in the future. When prices are rising, these professional investors will generally adjust their target upwards (to justify still owning the stock). However, as prices plateau, they reexamine their models. They become less willing to buy—it is much harder to justify purchases at the excessive valuation. Additionally, who is willing to sell as prices are rallying? Very few, because of the dynamics of performing against their benchmark that we described in Chapter 5. However, as prices begin to plateau and then start down in the Warning Phase, the incentive to book profits increases. If a stock had been rising as a result of increasing business—more sales, more profits—eventually those drivers start to flatten out (sales growth rates slow, competitors eat away at sales) and sellers start to appear.

As prices start to top out, a second factor kicks in, caused by the professional hedge funds. Remember our discussion about the short sellers, who make money when the market is declining? What do they have to do to make money? They sell short. They don't want to short while prices are still increasing, because they lose more money as the price rises. However, as prices start to flatten out and turn down, they are more willing to try to short during rallies. This is frequently what causes no new highs in the 60 period high/low channel (more about this shortly). In order to capture their profits, these traders have to buy.

Additionally, as prices start to top out, the sophisticated traders, those in the markets every day, start selling. The more prices go sideways, the more likely there will be traders selling the rallies toward the highs. This is what creates a level of resistance in the market—resistance levels being places where sellers appear and prices no longer rise.

To summarize, in the Warning Phase buying pressure is abating because there is no one left to buy. Selling interest is appearing. This selling interest may include short selling.

IDENTIFYING POTENTIAL TRADING CANDIDATES IN THE WARNING PHASE

There are several characteristics that stocks will exhibit if they are potential Warning Phase trading candidates. Stocks that do not meet these criteria do not qualify as potential candidates. We are training your eye to see what good potential candidates look like.

In the Warning Phase, the 60 period low indicator is frequently showing no new lows by being flat for some time. This is telling us that there have been no new lows recently. The 60 period high indicator is frequently flattening or declining, meaning there also have been no new highs for some time, or the highs have been declining (typical of a downtrend). Because an uptrend is defined as a series of higher highs, the fact that there have been no new highs for some time is the best evidence that the uptrend may be ending and a downtrend is beginning.

Look for the following characteristics in our indicators in the Warning Phase to identify potential trading candidates.

60 Period High/Low Channel

In the Warning Phase, frequently there will not have been any new highs for quite some time, which means the 60 period high indicator will have been going sideways for an extended period (Figure 6.2). Likewise, the

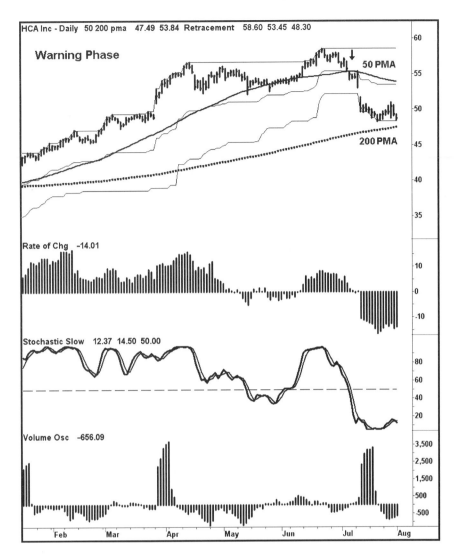

FIGURE 6.2 Warning Phase: HCA, Inc.

After a long, steady uptrend that started to consolidate, the close below the 50 PMA puts HCA into the Warning Phase (see down arrow). Also note that prices start to close below the 50 percent retracement area, something that they had never done during the previous phase, which is warning that there may be further weakness ahead. Additionally, when the Warning Phase begins, look at how narrow the channel has become—this illustrates extreme consolidation across the top, which makes the market vulnerable to a change in direction. Also note that the recent new high was of short duration—it was sold, not bought. Compare this to the new highs at the left of the chart where the uptrend was emerging. Shortly after entering the Warning Phase, price gapped to the downside, making new 60 period lows. Lower lows are what define a downtrend and confirm what the entry into the Warning Phase was signaling—that the uptrend was ending.

Source: © TradeStation Technologies, Inc. 1991–2005

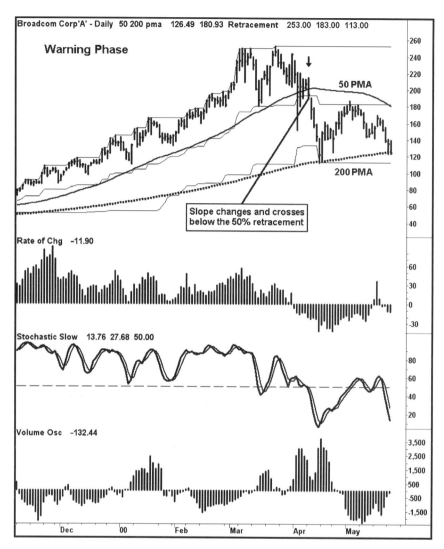

FIGURE 6.3 Warning Phase: Broadcom Corp.
As price penetrated the 50 PMA, BRCM entered the Warning Phase. Shortly thereafter, the slope of the 50 PMA changes from being up to down. This often provides
us with additional clues to a trend change. Note also that, upon entering the Warning Phase, prices started closing below the 50 percent retracement area for the
first time after an extended series of higher highs and higher lows. This is also signaling weakness.
Source: © TradeStation Technologies, Inc. 1991–2005

60 period low indicator may have been either going sideways or rising—if it is rising, this indicates that the lows are rising while the highs are not increasing. The channel will be narrowing. The lack of new highs is an excellent clue that the uptrend may be ending. Alternatively, there may have been a slight push into new highs that reversed and failed. If this is the case, traders and investors sold the new high, not bought it. Frequently, closes will be happening below the 50 percent retracement indictor. This means that closes are in the lower half of the channel, another warning clue that the up move may be ending, because strong stocks are usually closing above the 50 percent retracement indicator, in the upper half of the channel.

50 and 200 Period Moving Average

If the stock is truly topping out, the extended sideways action will result in a 50 PMA that is flattening out. The Warning Phase starts with closes below the 50 PMA. If the 50 PMA is flat when this happens, these lower closes will quickly start to drag the moving average down. Thus, as the Warning Phase progresses, the 50 PMA will start sloping down, as shown in Figure 6.3.

In the Warning Phase, the 50 PMA is above the 200 PMA. As the stock has been going sideways, the 200 PMA will have been catching up to the 50 PMA. It is likely that the 200 PMA is still rising, but it is also likely to be converging on the price and the 50 PMA, and the rate of its rise will be slowing.

Rate of Change Indicator

What characterizes the Warning Phase is the stock topping out—prices are no longer advancing and are starting to erode. This means that the Rate of Change indicator will be negative—prices are below where they were 21 periods ago (see Figure 6.4).

Stochastics

What characterizes the Warning Phase are closes below the 50 PMA—prices are going down. This means that closes will be in the lower part of the recent range; hence stochastics will be below the 50 percent mark (see Figure 6.5). Low stochastics are symptomatic of a market that is weakening.

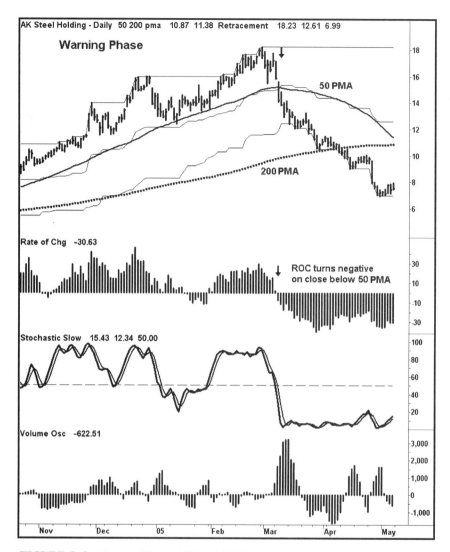

FIGURE 6.4   Warning Phase: AK Steel Holding
After an extended period of an uptrend with new highs, AKS closes below the 50 PMA, placing it in the Warning Phase. At this point the ROC momentum indicator moves below the zero line, telling us that the close at the break of the 50 PMA was less than that 21 bars ago. The start of negative momentum, prices selling off, clearly puts the sellers in charge as volume expands and price stairsteps lower.
Source: © TradeStation Technologies, Inc. 1991–2005

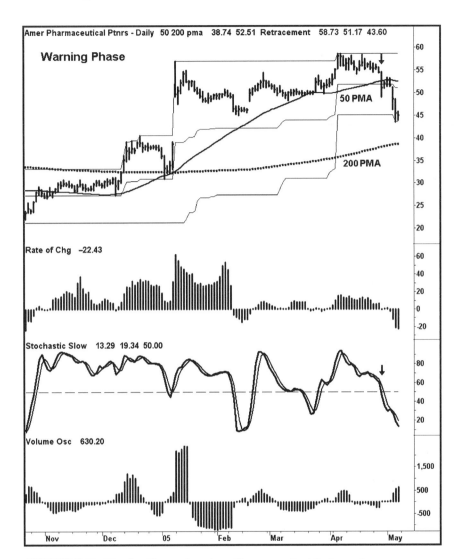

FIGURE 6.5 Warning Phase: American Pharmaceutical Partners, Inc.
As price crosses below the 50 PMA, placing this issue in the Warning Phase, stochastics move below the 50 zone. This alerts us that the close compared to its recent range is in the lower 50 percentile. These low readings, along with closes below the 50 percent retracement level of the 60 period high/low channel and the start of the downward slope of the 50 PMA, are symptomatic of a stock or any other financial instrument weakening.
Source: © TradeStation Technologies, Inc. 1991–2005

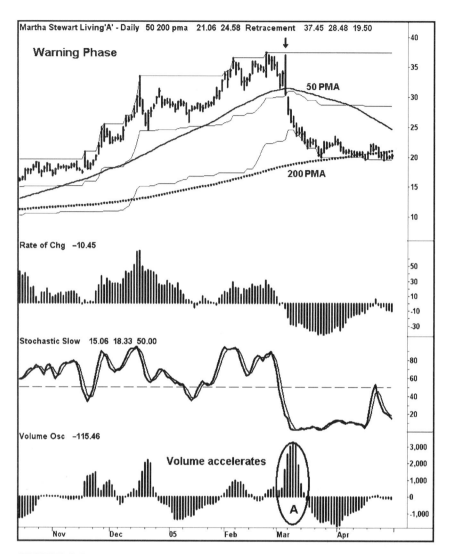

FIGURE 6.6 Warning Phase: Martha Stewart Living
At point A, volume accelerates as price crosses below the 50 PMA, which starts the Warning Phase (see down arrow). The increase in volume, coupled with lower prices, is telling us that selling pressure is increasing. With this volume expansion, price is also closing below the 50 percent retracement level. The ROC has also turned negative, and stochastics break below the 50 zone. Shortly thereafter, the 50 PMA starts sloping down, and new 60 period lows appear.
Source: © TradeStation Technologies, Inc. 1991–2005

Volume Oscillator

Because the Warning Phase is a result of investors and traders taking profits, volume is likely to be rising on the selloffs—traders are bailing out as prices start to fall (see Figure 6.6). The volume oscillator will be rising as prices move lower.

THE IDEAL WARNING PHASE CHARACTERISTICS

The best looking Warning Phase charts will have the characteristics shown in the following list. If these conditions are present, there is more likelihood of negative phase progression.

Sell Side	Warning Phase
50 PMA	Flat to sloping down
200 PMA	Sloping up
50% Retracement	At or below
60 period lower highs	Not required
60 period lower lows	Not required
Rate of Change	Begins to turn negative
Stochastic	Starts its move below the 50 zone
Volume oscillator	Above zero on the selloffs

The Ideal Warning Phase Chart

See Figure 6.7 on the following page.

Weekly Warning Phase Chart

This weekly chart (Figure 6.8) displays price expansion for more than 12 months.

Commodity: Daily Warning Phase Chart

This daily chart (Figure 6.9) provides us with clues to a trend ending.

Mutual Fund: Weekly Warning Phase Chart

Mutual fund investors can use the *TREND*advisor Diamond Analysis to make decisions about whether they should continue to hold a fund. (See Figure 6.10.)

The Ideal Warning Phase Chart

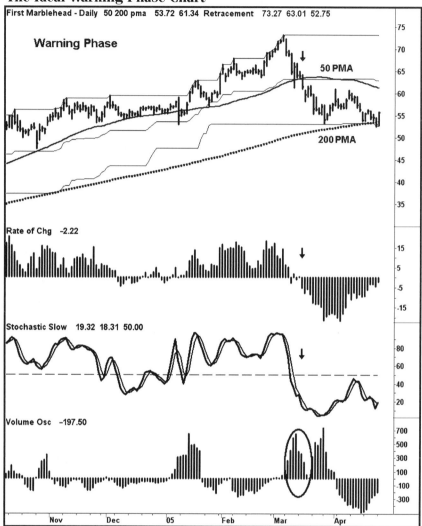

FIGURE 6.7   Warning Phase: First Marblehead
The components of an ideal Warning Phase chart are: no new 60 period highs; closing below the 50 PMA, which is often flat, or having a slight downward bias. Price is either at or below the 50 percent retracement area. The ROC is at or below the negative line and stochastics are nearing or below the 50 zone. Volume begins to accelerate as price makes lower lows.
Source: © TradeStation Technologies, Inc. 1991–2005

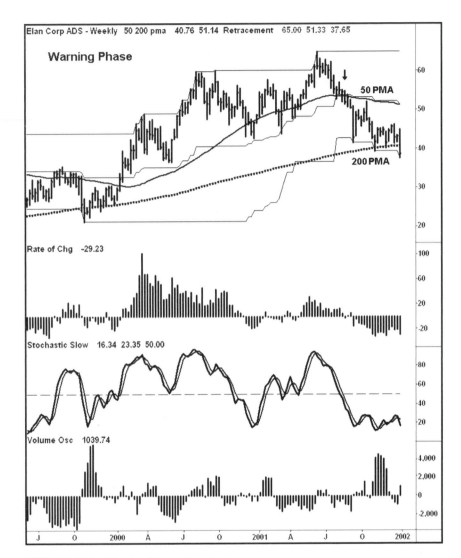

FIGURE 6.8 Warning Phase: Elan Corp.

After more than a year of price expansion, ELN met a sideways 50 PMA and closed below it and the 50 percent retracement area. The extended 60 period high channel and price making new 60 period lows set the stage for further erosion. This came with an ROC momentum indicator turning below the zero line and stochastics moving below the 50 zone.

Source: © TradeStation Technologies, Inc. 1991–2005

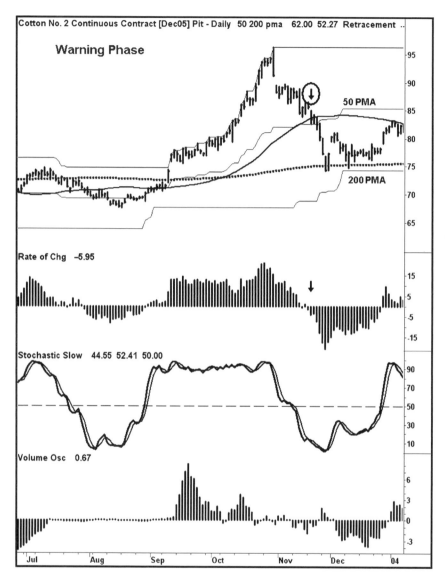

FIGURE 6.9 Warning Phase: Cotton

The Warning Phase provides us with the first clues to a potential end of a trend. The daily chart of cotton (at the arrow) shows price retracing 50 percent of its recent up move in a very short time frame. Once price closed below the 50 PMA, and the 50 percent retracement line, a quick burst to the support area at the 200 PMA followed. The ROC shows that negative momentum and low stochastics readings are describing the expansion of range to the downside, with closes near the lows, which are symptoms of weak financial instruments.

Source: © TradeStation Technologies, Inc. 1991–2005

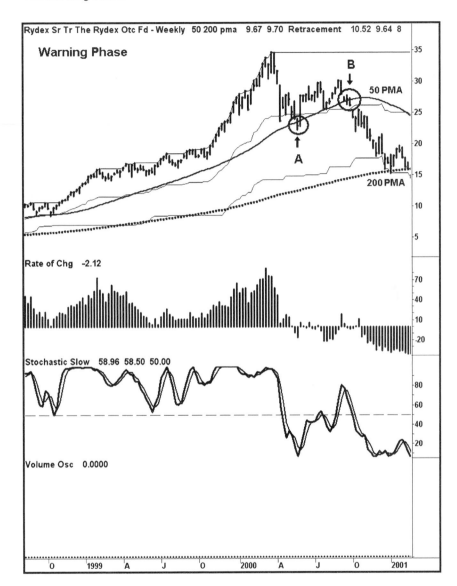

FIGURE 6.10 Warning Phase: Rydex OTC Fund

This fund had a very positive run, as shown by the positive ROC, new highs, and a sharp uptrend (from the left of the chart to the middle). But at point A, there was a successful test at the rising 50 PMA. Now, at point B, the 60 period high channel has been going sideways for some time, indicating no new highs, prices starting to close below the 50 PMA and the 50 percent retracement line. The ROC momentum has been flat to negative, which makes the instrument vulnerable to selling, which moves it clearly into negative territory. Often price will fall to the level of support at the 200 PMA.

Source: © TradeStation Technologies, Inc. 1991–2005

TRADING THE WARNING PHASE

If your stock or instrument is entering the Warning Phase, it is time to update (or develop) and execute your exit strategy for your long position. The most important action to take in the warning phase is to reduce your long exposure by paring back the size of the position you have.

When a market or stock first enters the Warning Phase by crossing below the 50 PMA, this is frequently an early indication that the preceding upward price action could be coming to an end. The Warning Phase is the first phase on the sell side of the *TREND*advisor Diamond. It is a phase in which to consider establishing new short positions because entry prices are generally high. The more trading criteria from the *TREND*advisor Diamond Matrix that the chart exhibits, the better the chances that a short trade may succeed (see the earlier Ideal Warning Phase Chart). However, the stock may not drop down right away, especially if there is still upward slope in the 50 PMA. Therefore, shorting (establishing a new short position) early in the Warning Phase is unwise for two reasons. The first is the probability of success is low—remember that even though current price is down, more recent price structure in the 50 PMA and longer term price structure in the 200 PMA are up. The trend is still up. So to short is to be fighting the more significant trend, which could resume and result in your taking a loss. The second reason to avoid going short early in a Warning Phase is the time it takes to make a return on your money. It takes time for a stock to deteriorate from an uptrend into a downtrend. If we short a stock early in the Warning Phase, our capital is tied up in something that is unlikely to earn us a decent return for a while. The likelihood of a decent return is low. To summarize, the risk is high and the likely return is low—not a good formula for success.

Before we talk about guidelines for trading the Warning Phase, let's review some principles of capital allocation in a portfolio that we discussed in detail in Chapter 3. Remember, it is important that your portfolio be diversified across a number of positions because the fewer positions you have, the more concentrated you are, which usually means more risk. Professional money managers are usually diversified across 10 or 20 positions at a minimum, and frequently more. Like the professional money managers, you also should be well diversified.

Trading tactics for this phase might include:

1. If you are going to establish new short positions in the Warning Phase, use one-third the capital of what would be your usual, normal position size. This does two things. First, a smaller position size means you will have less capital at risk if the stock goes against you and you get stopped out. Second, you will have less capital tied up in something that may take time to produce profits.

2. *Always* have a stop. Your stop should be a logical place on the chart where the trade is clearly failing. For short positions, this could include a close above the 50 PMA, which would constitute a phase failure.

3. The longer the Warning Phase goes on, the more evidence you will have of how it is likely to resolve. If you look at Figures 6.2 and 6.3, you will see that after these stocks first entered the Warning Phase, after the initial selloff, they consolidated before declining again. Waiting for more evidence before entering a short in the Warning Phase makes sense, because, as time goes on, more of the criteria for an ideal Warning Phase are met. Particularly, look for the 50 PMA to be flat when the phase begins and sloping down as the phase matures. Price should be at or below the 50 percent retracement line of the 60 period high/low channel. The Rate of Change indicator begins to turn negative and stochastics start to decline below the 50 zone. The volume oscillator crosses above zero, particularly on declines with new lows, thus indicating a pickup in volume. Look carefully at Figure 6.3, and note that after BRCM first entered the Warning Phase, it then bounced back up to the 50 percent retracement level of the high/low channel, where it failed. At the point where it hit the 50 percent retracement level of the high/low channel, note that the 50 PMA had rolled over and was beginning to slope down. There was better evidence for a potential short there than earlier. However, recognize that in strongly downtrending stocks like Figures 6.4 and 6.6, there is not much of a bounce—prices keep moving lower. If you short at these lower levels and your stop is above the 50 PMA, your stop will be quite wide.

4. *Always* have a plan to capture profits. At *TREND*advisor, we harvest part of the trade when it hits the first profit target, and then lower our stop on the remaining portion to the entry price. By using this as our methodology, we book profits on part of our position. For the remaining part, we protect ourselves from a loss by setting the stop at breakeven, while allowing for additional profits if the stock continues to decline.

5. If you are holding a long that enters the Warning Phase, it is potentially time to be exiting. The longer the stock has been topping out by going sideways, the potentially more significant the drop into the Warning Phase will be. Look at Figure 6.5. APPX had been going mostly sideways for five months before entering the Warning Phase. Note that the 60 period high/low channel had been contracting, evidence of narrowing range and a potential loss of the uptrend. Once this stock entered the Warning Phase, if you were long, it was time to reduce exposure and set your exit stop so if the stock fell further, you would be out.

THE END OF THE WARNING PHASE

The Warning Phase will end in one of two ways. It will either transition into the next downward phase (which would be good for our shorts), or it will fail with a close above the 50 PMA (which would mean a reentry back into the Bullish Phase).

A transition into the next downward phase (the Distribution Phase) is covered in Chapter 7, and is the best outcome for a short Warning Phase trade. However, as traders and investors, we have to be prepared that some of our trades will not work out. Our approach is to accept the reality that some things will not work and prepare you so you can identify what that looks like. Being prepared, knowing what to look for if something is not working, will help you to act. Too many of the traders and investors we work with show up with no understanding of what to do when things go against them, and get paralyzed into inaction. This exacerbates losses. It is far better to realize, and be prepared, that some things will not work, and to look for the signs of a Warning Phase failure, and have in your trading plan the action steps you will take if it materializes.

WARNING PHASE FAILURE CHART

It is not unusual for a stock to fail after it enters the Warning Phase for the first time (see Figure 6.11). If the price rallies back above the 50 PMA, this means the phase has failed. A Warning Phase failure is more likely if the 50 PMA is sloping up (price is fighting the recent trend), and the 200 PMA is also up. Rate of Change may be small (indicating very little momentum) but will become positive on the failure. Stochastics may be below 50, indicating that closes are in the lower region of the recent range, but there will be support there, and stochastics will quickly rise back up. There is a surge in volume. The surge of volume on the rally means there is buying interest in the stock.

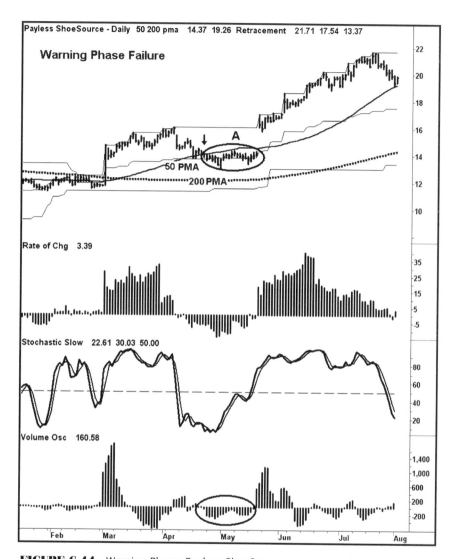

FIGURE 6.11 Warning Phase: Payless ShoeSource

As price makes its move into the Warning Phase (see the down arrow), a failure of this phase often is seen if the 50 PMA is upward sloping. At point A price moves sideways, with the ROC momentum indicator beginning to move from a negative to a positive. Stochastics, which have moved toward the lower boundary, now begin an upward move toward the 50 zone. Note that the change in the 200 PMA, the upward sloping 50 PMA, and the recent upward breakout of price from a very narrow, long consolidation, are all suggesting an emerging uptrend when the Warning Phase begins. Contrast this chart with those earlier in the chapter which show Warning Phases beginning after consolidations across tops, not out of bottoms as in this chart.

Source: © TradeStation Technologies, Inc. 1991–2005

CHAPTER 7

The Distribution Phase

The Distribution Phase is when investors and traders decide to liquidate their holdings (see Figure 7.1). Selling becomes more clearly pronounced. Evidence of emerging downtrend becomes apparent with lower lows and downward sloping moving averages.

As price begins to weaken or decline, we now have the current close of price below both the 50 PMA and the 200 PMA, but the relationship of the 50 PMA is still greater than the 200 PMA. In the Distribution Phase, the 50 PMA is still above the 200 PMA, which means that although price is weaker than both, there was sufficient recent action high enough for the 50 PMA to still be above the longer term average. The slope of the 200 PMA is losing shape. In this phase, there are frequently new lows made in the 60 period channel.

TRADING DYNAMICS OF THE DISTRIBUTION PHASE

The progression of how prices behave over time gives us insights into the dynamics of the changing nature of the forces of supply and demand—the forces of buyers and sellers interacting. The Distribution Phase is characterized by supply increasing.

We gave a more complete explanation of dynamics of supply and demand in Chapter 3. As a short summary: for every price that happens, there must be a buyer (creating demand) and a seller (creating supply). If there are sellers but no buyers, then prices must fall until buyers are induced into

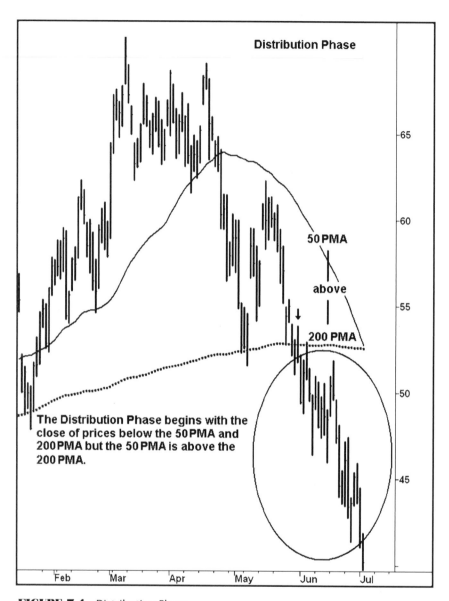

FIGURE 7.1   Distribution Phase
Source: © TradeStation Technologies, Inc. 1991–2005

buying. If there are buyers but not sellers, prices have to rise until sellers are induced to sell.

In the Distribution Phase, if prices are falling, one of several things must be happening. One possibility is that supply is staying the same, but demand is going down—if there are the same numbers of sellers for something but buyers stop buying (demand drops), then price will fall. If supply is increasing but demand stays the same, then prices will fall.

- Prices falling can be caused by supply staying the same but demand decreasing.
- Prices falling can be caused by supply increasing but demand staying the same.
- Prices falling can be caused by supply rising faster than demand.
- If prices are going sideways, then supply and demand are in balance.

In the Distribution Phase, generally selling pressure is rising. After a long period of consolidation and a series of declines, there now is more urgent selling. As prices start to drop, several things start happening.

Investors (mutual fund portfolio managers and other professional investors) are increasingly convinced that they should sell this instrument. If it is a stock, whatever the reasons that caused the previous rally, they are now deteriorating. Investors are much more willing to sell if they anticipate lower earnings. The Distribution Phase shows decreasing confidence in the stock. If the instrument is a commodity, there is a change in the underlying dynamics of demand (poor economic conditions in a particular country lead to less demand for the currency), or something is happening that anticipates an increase in supply (ideal weather conditions forecast in the midwest, which will lead to record crops).

As prices decline, a second factor kicks in. Remember our discussions about the short sellers, who make money when the market is declining? In order to make money, they have to sell short. They don't want to short while prices are rising because that creates losses. However, in the Distribution Phase, as the downtrend takes hold, they get more aggressive about selling short because it becomes easier to make money as the price continues down. Additionally, for the professional hedge fund managers who have been long, when prices start going sideways for a period of time, they are no longer making profits. In order to capture profits, they have to exit their longs. When prices start dropping in the Distribution Phase, their profits are quickly disappearing, so they are more eager to sell.

With prices declining, the sophisticated traders, those in the markets every day, decrease their buying and increase their selling. The more prices decline, creating a downtrend, the more likely there will be traders shorting at new lows. These traders are much less likely to be buying selloffs, which would give a floor to price. They are much more likely to be selling, creating additional supply.

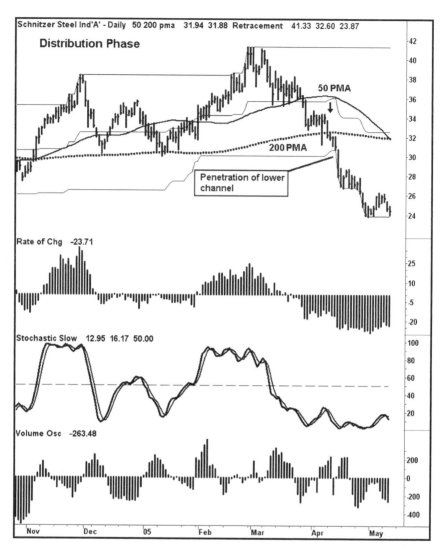

FIGURE 7.2 Distribution Phase: Schnitzer Steel

The Distribution Phase begins with price crossing below the 200 PMA, but the 50 PMA still above the 200 PMA (see down arrow). In this phase, price often makes new 60 period lows as seen in the chart above. These lower lows are what define a downtrend. Additionally, the ROC momentum is clearly negative, showing the negative percentage change of the current price from the price bar 21 periods ago (more than –20% at the right side of the chart).

Source: © TradeStation Technologies, Inc. 1991–2005

In short, in the Distribution Phase, selling pressure is increasing. As you can see, there are several groups who are starting to compete in selling—this is what drives prices lower.

IDENTIFYING POTENTIAL TRADING CANDIDATES IN THE DISTRIBUTION PHASE

The Distribution Phase is the start of downward price action; hence there will be lower lows and, frequently, lower highs. Thus, price will be pushing the 60 period low channel down and the 60 period high channel will be sideways or declining, as shown in Figure 7.2. These lower lows are characteristic of the beginnings of downward price action. Because the price action is along the 60 period low channel, obviously prices are below the 50 percent retracement line.

The decline in prices means that the 50 period moving average will be sloping down. As prices are now below the long term moving average, the 200 PMA will either be flattening out or also starting to slope down. As the Distribution Phase progresses, the longer prices stay below the 200 PMA, the more the 200 PMA will start to curl down.

Look for the following characteristics in our indicators in the Distribution Phase to identify potential trading candidates.

60 Period High/Low Channel

See Figure 7.2 on the facing page.

50 and 200 Period Moving Average

In the Distribution Phase, if the stock is truly starting a downtrend, the recent downward price action will result in a 50 PMA that is sloping down, as shown in Figure 7.3. The Distribution Phase starts with closes below the 200 PMA. This means that price has been sufficiently weak to drop below the longer term uptrend. If the 200 PMA is flat or declining slightly, this means that price has been going sideways, on average, for some time, which indicates a long topping pattern. If the 200 PMA is flat when prices start to close below it, these lower closes will quickly start to drag the moving average down. Thus, as the Distribution Phase progresses, look for the 200 PMA to start sloping down.

In the Distribution Phase, the 50 PMA is still above the 200 PMA. In a Distribution Phase that represents a long topping pattern, the 50 PMA and the 200 PMA will be converging. This setup is much better than a Distribution Phase where the 200 PMA is still sharply sloping up and the 50 PMA is far above the 200 PMA. In that circumstance, the price has moved sharply lower but is more likely to rally back than if the moving averages have

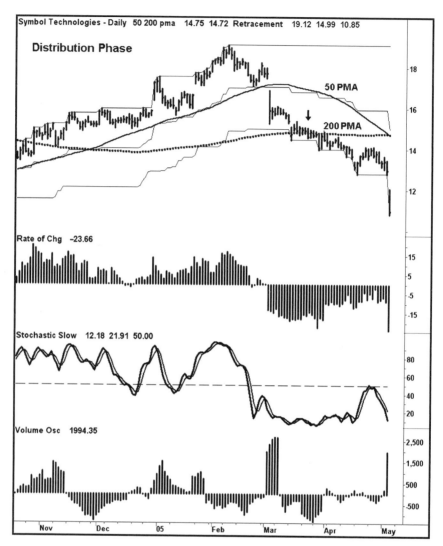

FIGURE 7.3 Distribution Phase: Symbol Technologies, Inc.
As price crosses below the flattening 200 PMA, SBL enters the Distribution Phase
(see down arrow). Also note that new 60 period lows are happening—lower lows
are what define a downtrend. The 50 PMA is clearly sloping down with price below
the 50 percent retracement area. This stairstepping of new 60 period lows shows
added selling pressure with each successive break.
Source: © TradeStation Technologies, Inc. 1991–2005

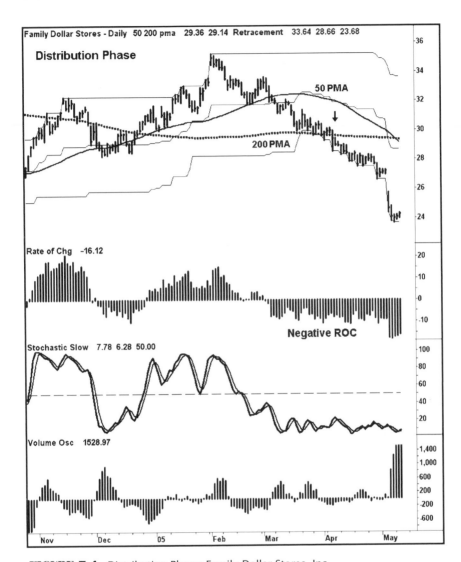

FIGURE 7.4 Distribution Phase: Family Dollar Stores, Inc.
As price closes below the 200 PMA starting the Distribution Phase (see down arrow), more signs of weakness are appearing. The ROC momentum has been below the zero line and continues to descend with each new low. The ROC accelerates further to the downside as price aggressively gaps down on an increase in volume. In downtrends, the negative ROC tells you the percentage of downward price change. Also note that there are new lows in the 60 period channel.
Source: © TradeStation Technologies, Inc. 1991–2005

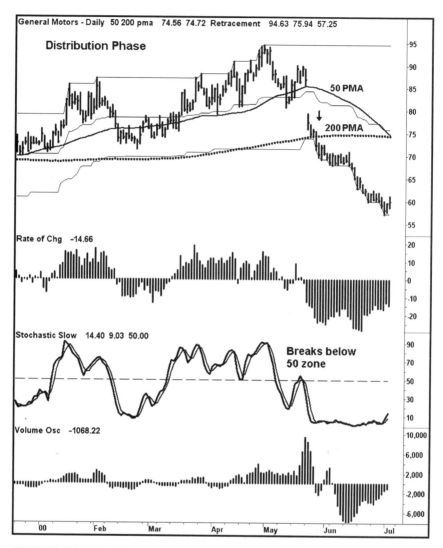

FIGURE 7.5 Distribution Phase: General Motors Corp.
With price closing below the 200 PMA and with a downward sloping 50 PMA, the
stage for weakness ahead is set (see down arrow). As new lows appear, they expand the range part of the stochastics calculation. Close low in that range pins the
indicator to the bottom. Readings near the low end of the scale tell us the closes
are weak, which is emblematic of downtrending financial instruments.
Source: © TradeStation Technologies, Inc. 1991–2005

converged and price has been in a long period of contraction. Think about it like a scale. The flatter the moving averages are early in the phase, the more likely lower prices will tip the averages down, which will turn on the sellers.

Rate of Change Indicator

The Rate of Change indicator will be persistently negative, showing that prices are almost always lower than they were 21 periods ago (see Figure 7.4 on page 133).

Stochastics

Because prices are going down, stochastics readings will be consistently low, staying below the 50 percent mark (see Figure 7.5). Remember that stochastics are measuring the close relative to the recent range. As prices decline into lower lows, it widens the range of the last 21 periods (see Chapter 1 for how stochastics are calculated). As prices close at the low, and those lows are lower as prices go down, the series of lower closes hugging the low range means that stochastic readings will be persistently low.

Volume Oscillator

A surge in the volume oscillator in the Distribution Phase as prices decline means that supply is overwhelming demand—more transactions are happening at lower prices, as shown in Figure 7.6. The rise in the volume oscillator confirms that there is significant selling pressure. However, on the sell side of the *TREND*advisor Diamond, prices can fall without any increase in volume. If the volume oscillator is increasing, that is confirmation that supply is overwhelming demand.

THE IDEAL DISTRIBUTION PHASE CHARACTERISTICS

The best looking Distribution Phase charts will have the characteristics shown in the following list. If these conditions are present, there is more likelihood of negative phase progression. (See Figure 7.7.)

Sell Side	Distribution Phase
50 PMA	Sloping down
200 PMA	Sideways with downward bias
50% Retracement	Price below
60 period lower highs	We begin to see 60 period lower highs
60 period lower lows	Price making new 60 period lower lows
Rate of Change	In negative territory
Stochastic	Is below the 50 zone
Volume oscillator	Above zero on the selloffs

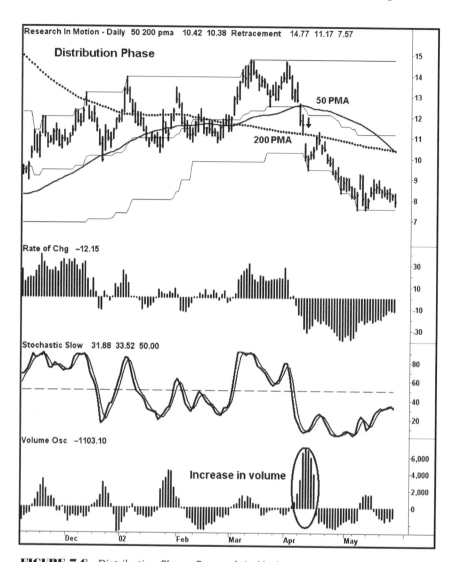

FIGURE 7.6 Distribution Phase: Research in Motion
As price gaps down into the Distribution Phase (see down arrow), volume increases and a new 60 period low is recorded. This volume surge demonstrates how the supply was overwhelming demand, thus causing the gap to new 60 period lows. This event is often driven by news or earnings announcements—the long term investors flee.
Source: © TradeStation Technologies, Inc. 1991–2005

The Ideal Distribution Phase Chart

See Figure 7.7 on the following page.

Weekly Distribution Phase Chart

This weekly chart (Figure 7.8) illustrates the components of the Distribution Phase.

Commodity: Weekly Distribution Phase Chart

The weekly chart of this commodity (Figure 7.9) displays the weakness in the Distribution Phase.

Mutual Fund: Weekly Distribution Phase Chart

The weekly chart of this mutual fund (Figure 7.10) provides clues into the Distribution Phase.

TRADING THE DISTRIBUTION PHASE

When stocks enter the Distribution Phase, the chances for further price declines get better. When the price first enters the Distribution Phase by closing below the 200 PMA, price is now lower than the longer term trend. This is potentially significant, particularly if the slope of the 200 PMA is flat or slightly declining after a long topping period. The Distribution Phase is the second phase on the sell side of the *TREND*advisor Diamond. It is a phase to consider when establishing additional short positions because trend is more in the investor's favor. The more trading criteria from the *TREND*advisor Diamond Matrix that the chart exhibits, the better the chances a short trade may succeed (see the earlier Ideal Distribution Phase Chart).

However, there is still risk of failure when the Distribution Phase begins because price has only recently declined below the longer term trend. Also, when price first enters this phase, there still may be some time before we have a profit. These two factors mean we should use less capital than a full position.

Before we talk about guidelines for trading the Distribution Phase, let's review some principles of capital allocation in a portfolio that we discussed in detail in Chapter 3. Remember, it is important that your portfolio be diversified across a number of positions because the fewer positions you have, the more concentrated you are, which usually means more risk. Professional money managers are usually diversified across 10 or 20 positions at a minimum, and frequently more. Like the professional money manager, you also should be well diversified.

The Ideal Distribution Phase Chart

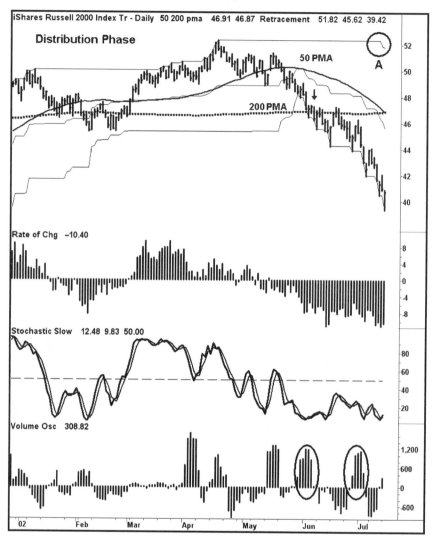

FIGURE 7.7 Distribution Phase: iShares Russell 2000 Value Index
The ideal Distribution Phase chart has these components: downward sloping 50 PMA; flattening 200 PMA; close below the 50 percent retracement channel; new 60 period lows being formed; ROC momentum negative; stochastics below 50; volume oscillator spikes with new lows. As the phase progresses, at point A we see the 60 period high channel starting to drop. A downtrend is a series of lower lows and lower highs. The channel is describing what can be seen in the price action.
Source: © TradeStation Technologies, Inc. 1991–2005

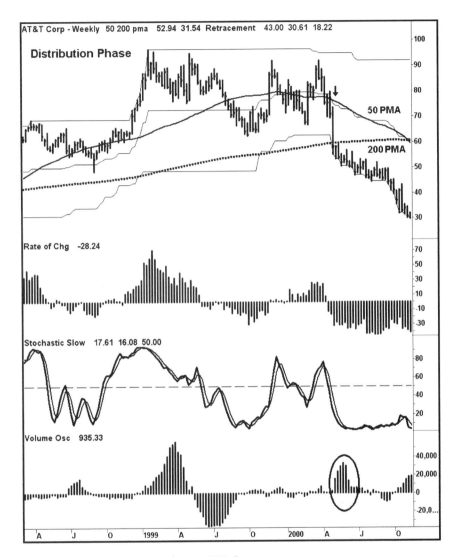

FIGURE 7.8 Distribution Phase: AT&T Corp.

The weekly chart of AT&T illustrates how components of the Distribution Phase can help longer term traders and investors. When price enters the phase at the down arrow, it happens concurrently with a new 60 period low. The ROC indicator quickly turns negative, and stochastics close near the bottom of the scale. The volume oscillator picks up the selling pressure as the oscillator expands above zero and the supply of stock outstrips the demand.

Source: © TradeStation Technologies, Inc. 1991–2005

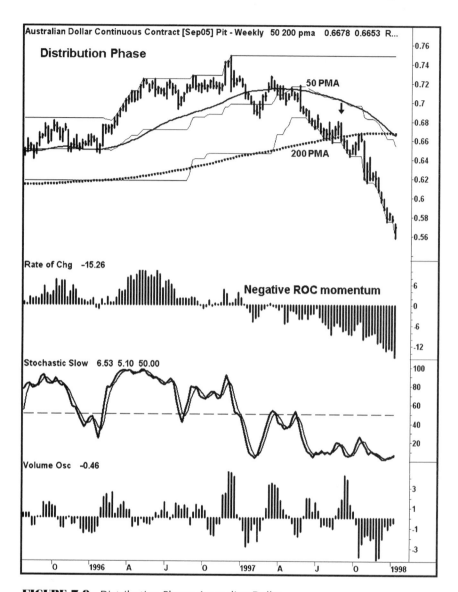

FIGURE 7.9   Distribution Phase: Australian Dollar

The weekly chart of the Australian Dollar shows the slide of this financial future. After the Distribution Phase begins (see the down arrow), price stairsteps lower, making new 60 period lower lows in the channel. The downward sloping 50 PMA and negative ROC momentum show that the sellers are in charge. Stochastics are pegged to the bottom of their range, closing in the lower 20 percent area, symptomatic of a downtrending instrument breaking to new lows.

Source: © TradeStation Technologies, Inc. 1991–2005

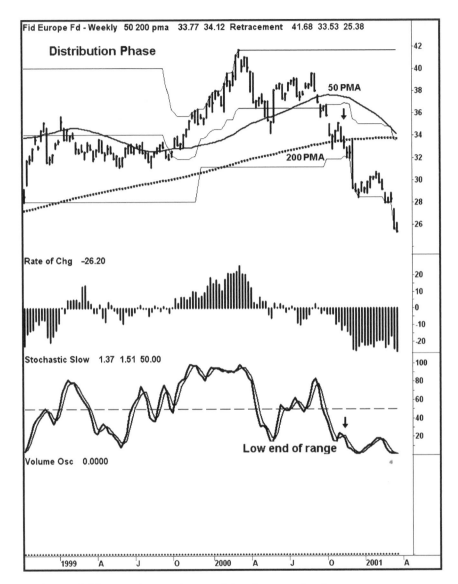

FIGURE 7.10 Distribution Phase: Fidelity European Fund

The weekly chart of the Fidelity European Fund provided clues before price broke into the Distribution Phase with the ROC being below zero. As price broke into the phase (see down arrow), there was a rapid decline in price with new 60 period lower lows being established. Stochastics continued to be in the lower 20 percent of their recent range.

Source: © TradeStation Technologies, Inc. 1991–2005

Trading tactics for this phase might include:

1. If you are going to establish a new short position in the Distribution Phase, use two-thirds the capital of what would be your usual, normal position size. This does two things. A smaller position size means you will have less capital at risk if the stock goes against you and you get stopped out. Also, you will have less capital tied up in something that may take time to produce profits.

2. *Always* have a stop. Your stop should be a logical place on the chart where the trade is clearly failing—for short positions, this could include a close above the 200 PMA, which would constitute a phase failure.

3. The longer the Distribution Phase goes on, the more evidence you will have of how it is likely to resolve. If you look at Figures 7.3, 7.6, and 7.7, you will see that after these stocks first entered the Distribution Phase, even if they sold off initially, they consolidated or bounced slightly before declining again. Entering part of the short early in the Distribution Phase may give you a favorable entry price, but waiting for more evidence before adding to it makes sense. Breaks to new lower lows, with declining moving averages later on in the phase, would confirm the downtrend. However, recognize that in strongly down trending stocks like those shown in Figures 7.2, 7.5, or 7.8, you will get lower prices for your shorts and, if your stop is above the 200, your stop will be quite wide. As time goes on, more of the criteria for an ideal Distribution Phase are met. Particularly, look for the 50 PMA sloping down. It is better if the 200 PMA is sideways, and best if it is sloping down. Price is below the 50 percent retracement line of the 60 period high/low channel. New 60 period lows should be occurring. The Rate of Change indicator is negative, stochastics are below the 50 zone and the volume oscillator is above zero, particularly on declines, thus indicating a pickup in volume.

4. *Always* have a plan to capture profits. At *TREND*advisor, we harvest part of the trade when it hits the first profit target, and then lower our stop on the remaining portion to the entry price. By using this as our methodology, we book profits on part of our position. For the remaining part, we protect ourselves from a loss by setting the stop at breakeven, while allowing for additional profits if the stock continues to decline.

5. Take no long positions in this phase.

THE END OF THE DISTRIBUTION PHASE

The Distribution Phase will end in one of two ways. It will either transition into the next downward phase or it will fail, with a close above the 200 PMA.

A transition into the next downward phase (the Bearish Phase) is covered in Chapter 8, and this is the best outcome for a short Distribution Phase trade. However, traders and investors have to be prepared that some trades will not work out. Knowing what to look for if something is not working will help you to act and not get paralyzed into inaction, which exacerbates losses. It is far better to look for the signs of a Distribution Phase failure and have in your trading plan the action steps you will take if it materializes.

DISTRIBUTION PHASE FAILURE CHART

It is not unusual for a stock to fail after it enters the Distribution Phase for the first time. If the price crosses back above the 200 PMA, this means the phase has failed. A Distribution Phase failure is more likely if the 200 PMA is sloping up (price is fighting the longer term trend), after a significant rally (see Figure 7.11 on the following page). The ROC is small (indicating very little negative momentum). Stochastics may be below 50, indicating that closes are in the lower region of the recent range, but they start rising. If there is an absence of volume on the down move, it indicates not much selling interest even though the price has declined. This further confirms the chances for failure.

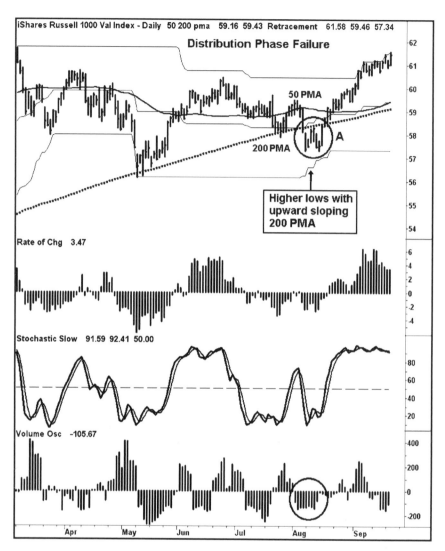

FIGURE 7.11 Distribution Phase: iShares Russell 1000 Value Index
A failure of the Distribution Phase is seen in IWD. Several characteristics that make
this likely to fail include: a strong upward sloping 200 PMA; price making 60 period higher lows, which is the opposite of this phase; and the absence of volume as
price declines. All these factors suggest that the decline into the Distribution Phase
might be nothing more than a pullback in an uptrend, which is confirmed when
price closes back above the 200 PMA at point A.
Source: © TradeStation Technologies, Inc. 1991–2005

CHAPTER 8

The Bearish Phase

The Bearish Phase is where heightened selling pressure ensues; everyone is trying to sell their stock—both the shorts as well as investors—which drives prices down sharply over time (see Figure 8.1).

Because short selling is such a force in downtrending stocks, let's review what it is from our discussion in the Introduction. Short selling is a tactic employed by sophisticated traders to profit from things that are going down, not up, in price. To conceptualize this, let's use a fictional story. Pretend that your analysis suggests that a company's stock is about to decline from its current price of $50 and you would like to profit from it. You call your friendly broker and tell him you would like to short 100 shares of the stock. He goes into his book of clients and finds a fellow who owns a bunch of this stock. He calls the fellow up and asks if the fellow would "lend" some of the stock and be paid some interest for lending it. The fellow says, "Let me see if I understand you. You would like to borrow some of my shares of stock. I will still own it. And you will pay me interest for lending it to you. Is that correct?" "Yes," replies the broker. "Okay." So the fellow lends the 100 shares to you. You take the borrowed 100 shares, sell them in the market for $50, and collect the proceeds ($5,000 less commissions, which you keep in your brokerage account). The stock falls to $40. The fellow calls the broker: "Remember the shares I lent you? I want them back now because I want to sell the stock." The broker calls you. "The lender wants his shares back." "No problem," you say. "Take some of the money in my account and buy 100 shares of stock at the current price of $40. Then return the 100 shares to the lender." Your broker does this. So you sold the borrowed 100 shares at $50, collecting $5,000. You bought

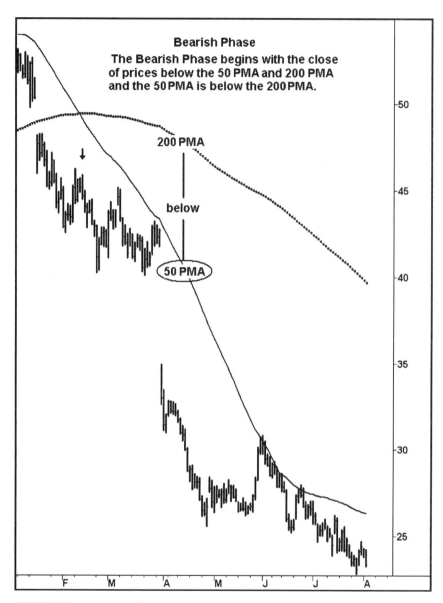

Bearish Phase
The Bearish Phase begins with the close
of prices below the 50 PMA and 200 PMA
and the 50 PMA is below the 200 PMA.

200 PMA

below

50 PMA

FIGURE 8.1 Bearish Phase
Source: © TradeStation Technologies, Inc. 1991–2005

back those sold shares at $40, for $4,000. The stock has gone down 10 points and you have made $1,000. Please note there are a number of substantial risks of shorting stocks, including, but not limited, to the company getting taken over and the stock price soaring. If the stock price goes up when you are short, you have losses because you have to buy back the stock at a higher price than you sold it for.

Because of these risks, short selling is only for sophisticated traders. However, it is widely used by hedge funds, which are extremely sophisticated. It is estimated that hedge funds control almost $1 trillion dollars, which is about the size of all mutual funds combined. Because of this, selling pressure in markets is not just from folks who own something selling it. Selling pressure in markets also includes short sellers. Short sellers are one of the significant reasons the Bearish Phase frequently shows the most pronounced selling.

In the Bearish Phase, price activity is the most negative of all the phases. The current close is less than both the 50 PMA and the 200 PMA but, most importantly, the relationship of the 50 PMA is less than the 200 PMA. This means that the current price is below recent trend and the recent trend is below the longer term trend. With this precise definition in place, the analyst, trader, or investor can then further examine the quality of instruments in a Bearish Phase. He should find, first, a series of lower lows in the 60 period channel combined with a downward sloping 50 PMA, which is below a downward sloping 200 PMA (both of which lag, but define this phase). Above all, continued new lows in the 60 period channel both confirm the downtrend as well as lead the 50 PMA and 200 PMA to continue down.

TRADING DYNAMICS OF THE BEARISH PHASE

As the phases on the sell side of the *TREND*advisor Diamond progress from Warning, to Distribution, to the Bearish Phase, we are getting insights into the dynamics of the changing nature of the forces of supply and demand—the forces of buyers and sellers interacting. The Bearish Phase is evidence of an almost complete lack of demand, and of supply overwhelming what little demand there is.

As a short summary about the dynamics of supply and demand from Chapter 3, for every price that happens, there must be a buyer (creating demand) and a seller (creating supply). If there are sellers but no buyers, then prices must fall until buyers are induced into buying. If there are buyers but no sellers, prices have to rise until sellers are induced to sell.

In the Bearish Phase, if prices are falling, one of several things must be happening. One possibility is that supply is staying the same, but demand is going down—if there are the same number of sellers for something, but buyers stop buying (demand drops), the price will fall. If supply is increasing, but demand stays the same, then prices will fall.

- Prices falling can be caused by supply staying the same but demand decreasing.
- Prices falling can be caused by supply increasing but demand staying the same.
- Prices falling can be caused by supply rising faster than demand.
- If prices are going sideways, then supply and demand are in balance.

In the Bearish Phase, what is generally going on is that selling pressure is so strong, and buyers are so sporadic, that prices are either declining sharply or consolidating at low levels after a drop. Particularly in the early and mid parts of the Bearish Phase, supply is huge and there is little demand. With prices falling, several things are happening.

Investors (mutual fund portfolio managers and other professional investors) are completely convinced that they should sell this instrument. If it is a stock, the conditions that were driving the earnings are so awful that it is obvious to all the investors that they do not want to own this name. Investors are not willing to buy—there are no reasons to own the stock—no new products, the economy is lousy, management can't increase profits. The Bearish Phase shows no confidence in the stock. There is an additional dynamic going on in the Bearish Phase with the professional investors. As we have previously discussed, the mutual fund portfolio managers are paid on the performance of their portfolio relative to its benchmark index. Many managers try to beat the benchmark index by overweighting, or owning more of, the stocks they think will be good performers. If a stock is overweighted in their portfolio, and it starts to decline sharply, the benchmark index will start to outperform the portfolio manager's fund. This forces the manager into selling the stock—if he doesn't cut it back or get rid of it in his portfolio, the benchmark index will continue to outperform him, and he will lose his bonus or his job. Remember, these professional investors cannot short. They have to own stocks. In selloffs, they are trying to guess what will hurt them the least. This dynamic of having to sell out of a name that is underperforming is part of the fuel of declines in the Bearish Phase. If the instrument is a commodity, there is a change in the underlying dynamics of demand, or something is happening to cause a sharp increase in supply (record orange juice crops in both Florida and Brazil, for example).

As prices decline, a second factor kicks in. The professional short sellers, who make money when the market is declining, become increasingly aggressive. They understand that the mutual fund and other professional investors, who have to own stocks, have only a limited amount of cash that can be spent to buy as prices decline. There are few buyers, so prices drop quickly. This creates a great incentive for the shorts to sell. One of the dynamics in the Bearish Phase is that there are very few traders willing to buy into the decline. They don't want to buy while prices are going down, because those purchases lose money as prices go down. The traders and hedge funds who get paid on absolute performance do not want losers because their paychecks get cut. This leads to an absence of demand in the Bearish Phase.

Additionally, with prices declining, the sophisticated traders, those in the markets every day, decrease their buying. The more prices sell off, creating a downtrend, the more likely there will be traders shorting breakdowns at new lows and selling the rallies. These traders are much less likely to be buying selloffs, which would put a floor under price, at least early on in the Bearish Phase. They are much more likely to be selling, creating underlying supply.

However, as the Bearish Phase matures, one of the things to look for is a willingness of traders to start to buy at support, buying where buyers have shown up before. We will look at this in more detail later in the chapter.

In short, in the Bearish Phase, selling pressure is high. Perhaps even more importantly, there are very few buyers. As you can see, there are several groups who are competing in selling and very few willing to buy— this is what causes prices to drop sharply, particularly early in the phase.

IDENTIFYING POTENTIAL TRADING CANDIDATES IN THE BEARISH PHASE

There are several characteristics that stocks will exhibit if they are potential Bearish Phase trading candidates. Stocks that do not meet these criteria do not qualify to be potential candidates. We are training your eye to see what good potential candidates look like.

In the Bearish Phase, the 60 period low indicator is frequently indicating lower lows by dropping. This is telling us that there is a series of new lows. The 60 period high indicator is frequently dropping, meaning that highs are declining. Because a downtrend is defined as a series of lower lows with lower highs in between, new lows in the 60 period channel are the best evidence of the downtrend extending.

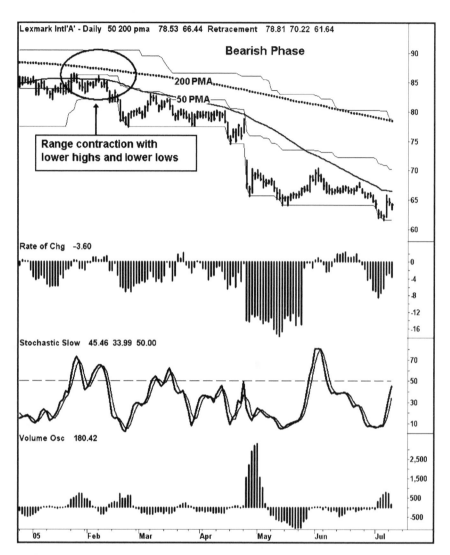

FIGURE 8.2 Bearish Phase: Lexmark International "A"
Range contraction in the 60 period high/low channel often precedes price expansion. The instrument has come to a place of equilibrium where it can be tilted one way or the other. All that is needed is the evidence to determine the direction of that price expansion. The first clue to the price direction is the downward sloping 200 PMA—this means the long term trend is down. Next, the 50 PMA is rolling over. Price is in the lower half of the 60 period high/low channel. As price penetrates the 60 period low, the snowball effect takes place with the ROC turning negative. Then stochastics begin their decline below the 50 zone. Finally, volume accelerates on the push downs, showing selling overwhelming the few buyers there are, and abates on the push ups, indicating lack of demand.
Source: © TradeStation Technologies, Inc. 1991–2005

The Bearish Phase is when prices are trending sharply down over time. The Bearish Phase is characterized by:

- A series of lower lows and lower highs
- Downward sloping moving averages
- Powerful negative momentum (larger down price moves in short time frames)
- Stochastics below 50 zone
- Accelerating volume

Look for the characteristics described in the next five sections as indicators in the Bearish Phase to identify potential trading candidates.

60 Period High/Low Channel

Downtrend is what the Bearish Phase shows. Downtrends are defined by lower lows. Therefore, in the Bearish Phase, one should see lower lows in the 60 period low channel in a progression of step-downs (see Figure 8.2). Likewise, in a downtrend, frequently there will be lower highs. The 60 period high channel will be stepping down as well. In a downtrend, prices will usually be closing in the lower end of the channel. Therefore, most price action will be below the 50 percent retracement.

50 and 200 Period Moving Average

In the Bearish Phase, the 50 PMA will be sloping down, following the price action, which is going down. The 50 PMA will be below the 200 PMA (see Figure 8.3). Also, the 200 PMA should be sloping down, which is showing the long-term price trend is down. By the time the Bearish Phase has started, prices have been declining through the progression from Warning Phase to Distribution Phase to Bearish. The progression of lower prices over time is what causes the 200 PMA to slope downwards.

Rate of Change Indicator

In the Bearish Phase, the Rate of Change indicator will be consistently negative; this shows that prices are persistently lower than the 21 period lookback (see Figure 8.4).

Stochastics

As prices drop into lower lows, the range component of stochastics widens (see Figure 8.5). This, combined with the closes at the low end of

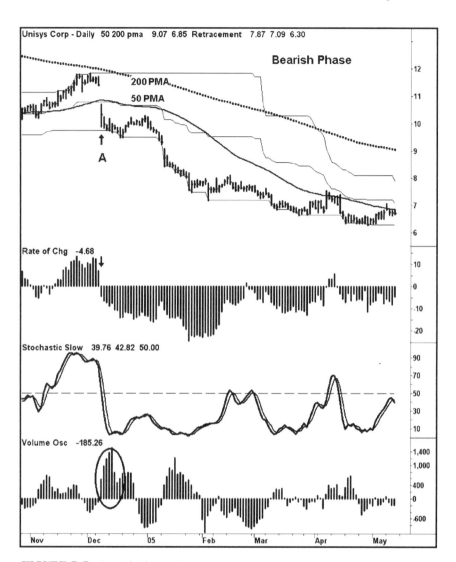

FIGURE 8.3   Bearish Phase: Unisys Corp.

At point A price moves into the Bearish Phase with a downward sloping 200 PMA, suggesting further price weakness ahead. As the phase progresses, the slope of the 50 PMA turns strongly to the downside. The ROC gets increasingly negative on the selloffs, showing the percent moves over 21 periods. Stochastics stay pegged below the 50 zone, which shows that closes are consistently in the lower half of the recent range, which is typical of weak stocks and other weak financial instruments. The volume oscillator shows volume expansion as price declines and the absence of volume as price moves up.

Source: © TradeStation Technologies, Inc. 1991–2005

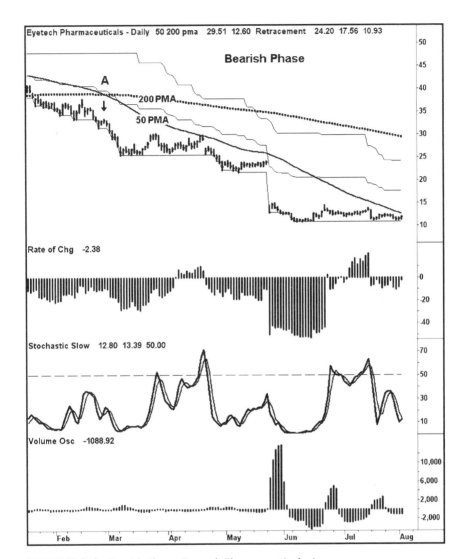

FIGURE 8.4 Bearish Phase: Eyetech Pharmaceuticals, Inc.
This example shows the 50 PMA crossing the 200 PMA, which is what triggers
EYET into the Bearish Phase—price was already below the 50 PMA and the 200 PMA
(see down arrow). As prices step lower and lower, that pulls down the slope of
both the 50 and 200 PMAs. Note what happens on the weak rallies in a Bearish
Phase. For example, in April the ROC moved above zero and stochastics moved
above the 50 zone. When price met the downward sloping 50 PMA, sellers appeared. These patterns show the excellent shorting opportunities traders take advantage of as price pulls up in a downtrend.
Source: © TradeStation Technologies, Inc. 1991–2005

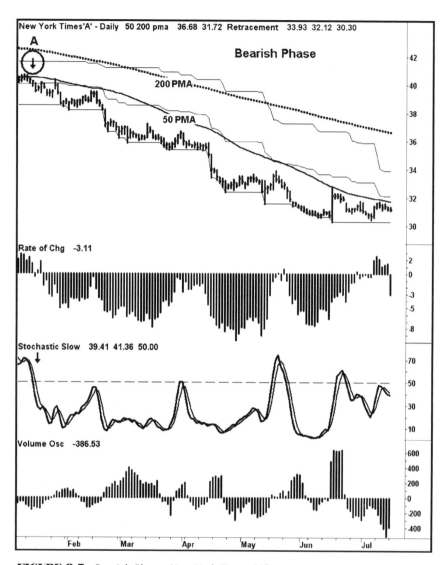

FIGURE 8.5 Bearish Phase: New York Times "A"

At point A price moves into the Bearish Phase with closes below the 50 PMA (see arrow in the circle). At this time, stochastics cross below the 50 zone (see down arrow on the stochactic indicator), which is showing the weakening of price with closes in the lower half of recent range. Additionally, price is closing below the 50 percent retracement line of the 60 period high/low channel, more evidence of weakness. The downward sloping 50 and 200 PMA, with a break into new lows, begin the extended slide.

Source: © TradeStation Technologies, Inc. 1991–2005

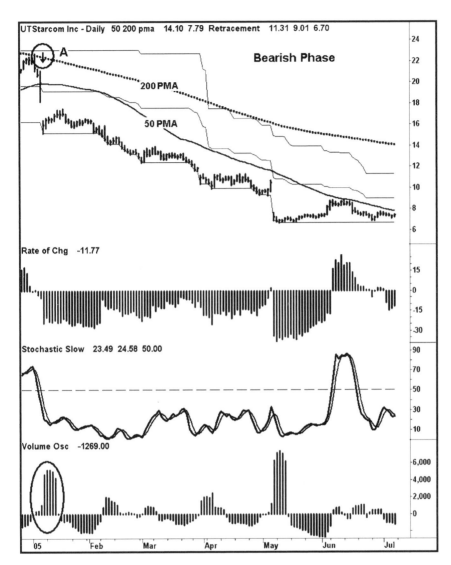

FIGURE 8.6 Bearish Phase: UT Starcom, Inc.
Common to the Bearish Phase are gaps to the downside on increased volume. Point
A price moves into the Bearish Phase with an increase in volume. As price declines
and the phase progresses, in May there is another gap to the downside with an in-
crease in volume.
Source: © TradeStation Technologies, Inc. 1991–2005

the range that is emblematic of downtrends, means stochastics readings will be persistently low and almost always below 50 percent.

Volume Oscillator

In the Bearish Phase the volume oscillator will go positive on the sell-offs, which means that volume is surging as prices break lower (see Figure 8.6 on previous page). However, on the sell side of the *TRENDadvisor* Diamond, prices can fall without any increase in volume. If the volume oscillator is increasing, that is confirmation that supply is overwhelming demand.

THE IDEAL BEARISH PHASE CHARACTERISTICS

The best looking Bearish Phase charts will have the characteristics shown in the following list. If these conditions are present, negative phase progression is more likely.

Sell Side	Bearish Phase
50 PMA	Sloping down
200 PMA	Sloping down
50% Retracement	Price below
60 period lower highs	Price making new 60 period lower highs
60 period lower lows	Channel making 60 period lower lows
Rate of Change	In negative territory
Stochastic	Is below the 50 zone
Volume oscillator	Above zero on the selloffs

The Ideal Bearish Phase Chart

See Figure 8.7 on the following page.

The Ideal Bearish Phase Chart

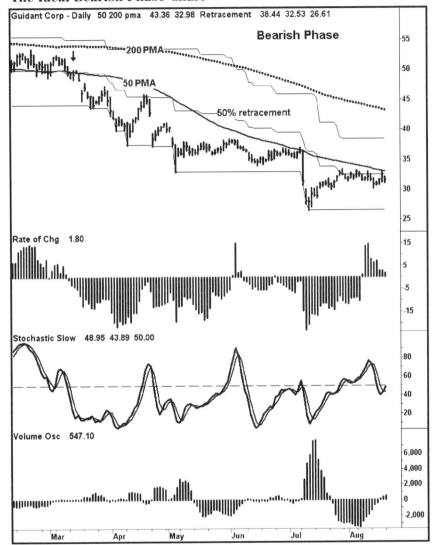

FIGURE 8.7 Bearish Phase: Guidant Corp.

The ideal Bearish Phase chart exhibits these characteristics: a downward sloping 50 and 200 PMA, which means both the recent and longer term trends are down; price makes new 60 period lower lows and 60 period lower highs in the channel; price stays below the 50 percent retracement of the channel; The ROC momentum is negative, telling us the close of price is lower than 21 bars ago; stochastics are in the lower half of the zone, persistently below 50; pullups are met with selling, which shows how traders take advantage of shorting opportunities; the volume oscillator increases above zero on the selloffs and does not rally much on the pushups.

Source: © TradeStation Technologies, Inc. 1991–2005

Weekly Bearish Phase Chart

The weekly Bearish Phase chart (Figure 8.8) displays the selling pressure of this phase.

Commodity: Weekly Bearish Phase Chart

The weekly chart of this commodity (Figure 8.9) exhibits the downside potential of the Bearish Phase.

Mutual Fund: Weekly Bearish Phase Chart

The weekly chart of this mutual fund (Figure 8.10) displays the fierce selling pressure of the Bearish Phase.

TRADING THE BEARISH PHASE

When stocks enter the Bearish Phase, the chances for further price declines get better. When the Bearish Phase begins with price below the 50 PMA and 200 PMA, and the 50 PMA is below the 200 PMA, current trend is down; recent trend (as evidenced by the 50 PMA) is below long term trend (as evidenced by the 200 PMA). This is potentially significant because it indicates the potential for further, powerful down moves. The Bearish Phase is the third phase on the "sell side" of the *TREND*advisor Diamond. It is a phase in which to consider establishing additional short positions because trend is in our favor. The more trading criteria from the *TREND*advisor Diamond Matrix that the chart exhibits, the better the chances a short trade may succeed (see the earlier Ideal Bearish Phase Chart).

As the Bearish Phase begins, particularly if the ideal criteria are met, the chances for success of short trades are very good. Therefore, this is a phase for considering using a full capital position.

Before we talk about guidelines for trading the Bearish Phase, let's review some principles of capital allocation in a portfolio that we discussed in detail in Chapter 3. Remember, it is important that your portfolio be diversified across a number of positions because the fewer positions you have, the more concentrated you are, which usually means more risk. Professional money managers are usually diversified across 10 or 20 positions at a minimum, and frequently more. Like the professional money managers, you also should be well diversified. Do not become overconcentrated in any one or even a few positions.

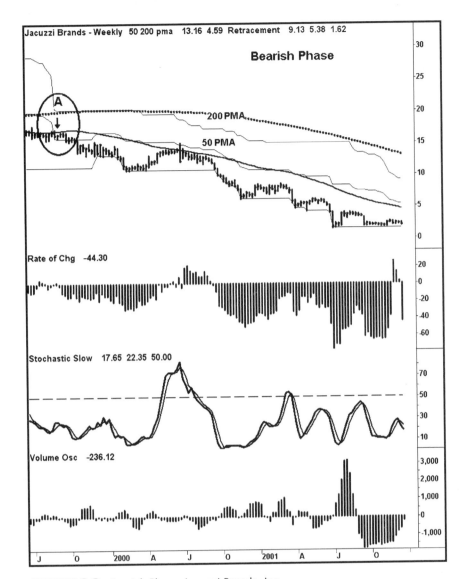

FIGURE 8.8 Bearish Phase: Jacuzzi Brands, Inc.

The weekly Bearish Phase chart displays how a stock progresses in this phase. At point A, JJZ moves into the Bearish Phase when price closes below the 50 PMA (the 50 PMA is already below the 200 PMA). Both the 50 and 200 PMA are flat. Combined with the 60 period high/low channel contracting, this stock is in relative equilibrium and vulnerable to a price change forthcoming. Once the lower lows appear in early 2000, the downtrend is confirmed. In June of 2000, price rebounds. On that pushup, the stochastics indicator surges with a move to the upper 80 percent of its recent range—note, however, how narrow that range is, and the ROC turns positive. The pushup meets with selling when price hits the 50 percent line of the 60 period high/low channel and the downward sloping 50 PMA. This sets the stage for the weakness ahead, which is confirmed when price breaks into new lows later that year.

Source: © TradeStation Technologies, Inc. 1991–2005

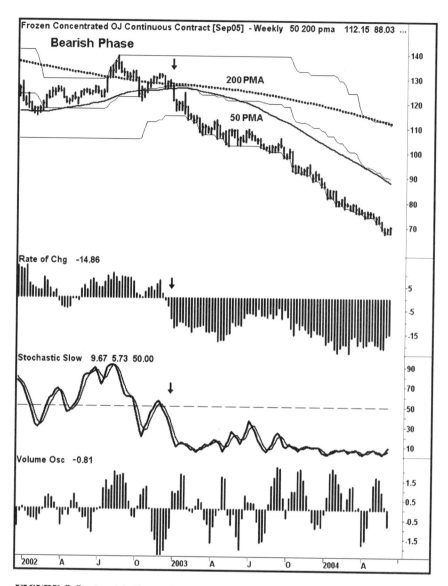

FIGURE 8.9 Bearish Phase: Frozen OJ

The weekly chart of OJ exhibits the downside potential of the Bearish Phase. All indicators are moving in sync. At the arrow, the 60 period high/low channel was contracting, but prices were closing below the 50 percent retracement line. The ROC had turned negative. Stochastics dropped below the 50 zone. As soon as the new lows appeared, the sellers took charge. The downward sloping 200 PMA was a tipoff to the imminent price declines forthcoming.

Source: © TradeStation Technologies, Inc. 1991–2005

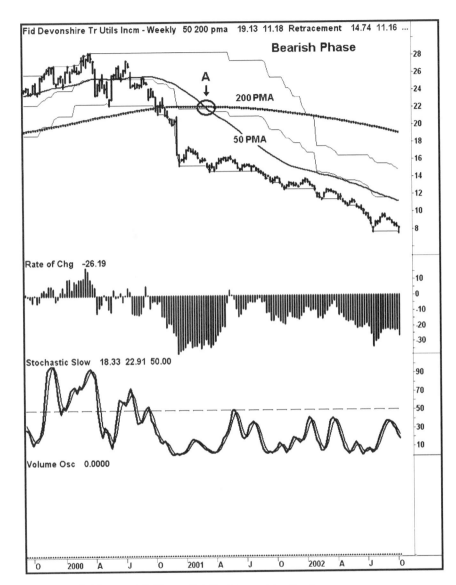

FIGURE 8.10 Bearish Phase: Fidelity Devonshire Trust

The Bearish Phase was triggered when the 50 PMA crossed below the 200 PMA (the price was already below both). Once this unfolded, fierce selling took place, pushing this fund into single digits. The ROC momentum and stochastics were persistently low, exhibiting the dynamic of no demand in the downtrend.

Source: © TradeStation Technologies, Inc. 1991–2005

Trading tactics for this phase might include:

1. If you are going to establish new long positions in the Bearish Phase, consider a full, normal position size.

2. *Always* have a stop. Your stop should be a logical place on the chart where the trade is clearly failing—for short positions, this could include a close above the 50 PMA, which would constitute a phase failure.

3. The longer the Bearish Phase goes on, the more evidence you will have of how it is resolving. It may be better to enter your position early in the phase as long as the criteria for an ideal Bearish Phase are met. Early entry means you will have profits as the phase progresses, if price continues to trend down. In order to enter, look for the 50 PMA to be sloping down; the 200 PMA also should be sloping down. Price is below the 50 percent retracement line of the 60 period high/low channel. The 50 percent retracement line must be declining, and there should be new 60 period lows and lower 60 period highs. The Rate of Change indicator is negative; stochastics are persistently below the 50 zone and frequently quite low. In the Bearish Phase, the volume oscillator very often declines on consolidations, indicating light volume on pullups. On declines, particularly as price breaks to new lows, it should move above zero to indicate a pickup in volume. Late in the Bearish Phase, a sign of its potential tiring is that there is no surge of volume on the declines.

4. *Always* have a plan to capture profits. At *TREND*advisor, we harvest part of the trade when it hits the first profit target, and then lower our stop on the remaining portion to the entry price. By using this as our methodology, we book profits on part of our position. For the remaining part, we protect ourselves from a loss by setting the stop at breakeven, while allowing for additional profits if the stock continues to decline.

5. Take no long positions in this phase.

There are a variety of ways to trade the Bearish Phase but we will focus on two: shorting the breakdowns (selling weakness), or selling the consolidations (selling strength in underlying weakness). The conditions and rules presented below are based on daily chart analysis.

At *TREND*advisor, our focus is on shorter term trading—our positions are on for only a matter of days. Given that this is our objective, our *TREND*advisor Diamond Trading Methodology is based on:

- Opportunities that can produce 3 percent to 7 percent on any one trade, based on our plan. For longer-term investors, clearly your objective will be higher.
- Stop orders to exit and enter at points specified by the methodology.

Each trade complies with specified rules in the plan objectives and plan strategy and reflects sound money management. The Bearish Phase is becoming more popular as investors and traders develop their skills in shorting stocks. This phase is often the start of a major downtrend. Some of its characteristics are:

- Price declines on the short side are fast and furious.
- Volume accelerates as new lows are being made.
- Sellers become aggressive.
- Breakaway price gaps occur often, usually on heavier volume.

Bearish Phase Conditions

- Price closes are below the 50 period moving average.
- Price closes are below the 200 period moving average.
- 50 period moving average is below the 200 period moving average.

Shorting financial instruments when the above criteria are met often leads to safe opportunities over all time frames. However, when holding a short on a security for an extended period of time, a sound trading and money management plan should be deployed. This increases your chances for success.

The criteria for selling weakness in the Bearish Phase are:

- Price is breaking down to new 60 period lows.
- The 50 and 200 moving averages are sloping down or the last period is less than the previous period.
- The Rate of Change indicator is below the zero line and accelerating to the downside (this tells us we have negative momentum).
- The stochastics indicator is below the 50 zone and declining (this tells us we are closing in the bottom 50 percent of our defined range).
- Volume is increasing as the volume oscillator moves above the zero line (this tells us the short term moving average of volume is expanding above the longer term moving average).

Rules for Short Entry

Screen stocks that meet the above criteria. Open a position on the *short side*: Short when the stock price trades one-eighth to three-eighths below yesterday's low (the 1/8 to 3/8 range should be based on price and volatility of the stock).

Rules to Exit

Initial stop: Your stop should be a logical place on the chart where the trade is clearly failing. For short positions, this could include a close above the 50 PMA, which would constitute a phase failure.

Always harvest profits: Buy in, or cover, half of the short position at a target price objective, based on your trading plan, and then manage the remaining half of the position. As price moves lower, place a trailing buy stop at the entry price and let the price move continue down (or up) until the price stops at last target.

Buy to cover the short at less than target when price (volume) stalls (see Bearish Phase Failure). Buy to cover the remaining position when the phase changes.

RULES TO TRADE

Trade with the Market

Stock candidates should be chosen carefully. This should be based on the investor's plan objective and risk tolerance. Trading with the market allows the investor or trader the benefits of market momentum. Candidates with high deltas in a Bearish Phase also increase an investor's winning percentages (high delta or high beta is when an individual stock outperforms the market).

Trade with the Sectors

We use the acronym MSE, meaning trade in the direction of the Market first, followed by the Sector, and then use a top down approach to those Equities meeting your criteria. The market is the engine that pulls along the sectors and the equities. When we have this all in sync the likelihood of trading success is greatly enhanced.

Shorting Pullups

In the Bearish Phase, prices often move to the downward sloping 50 period moving average, offering an excellent shorting opportunity. Prices will also move to a 50 percent retracement of the 60 period high/low channels. Volume will very often be lighter on these pullups because sellers are unwilling to give up the price of the security at the higher levels, suggesting weakness. Entries in the Bearish Phase should be timed with the overall market and accompanying industry sector. Therefore, if the market and industry sectors are declining and in the Bearish Phase, look for stocks that are in the Bearish Phase. Taking it one step further, the investors and traders who shorted in the Warning Phase are probably looking to harvest a portion of their profits but not willing to give up the full position. This is why volume is often lighter on these pullups and the overall trend is still down.

Conditions to Short in Bearish Phase

- Price breaking below a declining 50 PMA.
- Price stalls at the 50 percent retracement level of the 60 period high/low channel.
- Price breaks down to new 60 period lows.
- The Rate of Change indicator moves down through the zero line, suggesting a decline in momentum.
- Stochastics move below the 50 zone, telling us the close is in the lower 50 percent of the recent range.
- Volume oscillator breaks above the zero line; this supports near term shorting interest.

Bull Fake Shorting Opportunity

The Bull Fake is a bearish selling opportunity. The setup unfolds by: first scouting for a price close above a downward sloping 50 PMA; price is below the downward sloping 200 PMA and the 50 PMA is below the 200 PMA. This alerts us to a potential Bull Fake shorting opportunity. Once the above conditions have been met, we then watch for price to close below the downward sloping 50 PMA, usually within one to six periods. This triggers the short and a short position is then established. What actually takes place is that price reverses from the Bearish Phase to the Recovery Phase, and then reverts back into the Bearish Phase, usually within one to six periods; this is nothing more than a pullup in a downtrend. See Figures 8.11 and 8.12 as examples.

Characteristics of Bull Fake Setups

- Downward sloping 50 and 200 PMA.
- Lower lows and lower highs in the 60 period high/low channel.
- Price below the 50 percent retracement level of the 60 period high/low channel.
- The Rate of Change indicator is below the zero line, suggesting a decline in momentum.
- Stochastics are below the 50 zone, telling us the close is in the lower 50 percent of the range.
- Volume oscillator is above the zero line; this supports near term selling interest.
- Time your entries with a declining market and declining sector.

Goodyear Tire & Rubber—Bull Fake Strategy

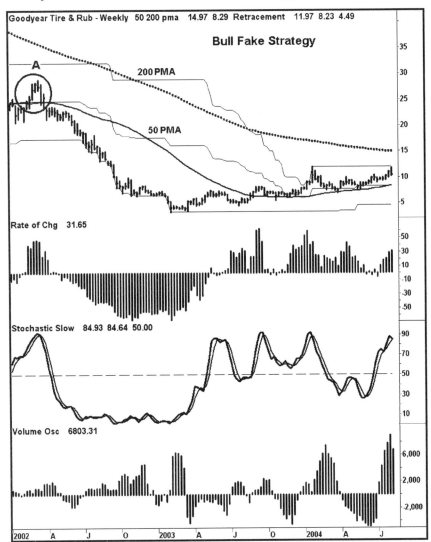

FIGURE 8.11 Bull Fake Strategy: Goodyear Tire & Rubber

The Bull Fake strategy is a very powerful setup when all characteristics are in place. First we scout for price moving above the downward sloping 50 PMA with a downward sloping 200 PMA, as seen at point A. The key to this setup is having price be above the 50 PMA for one to six periods. We then watch for price closing below the 50 PMA while taking out the prior bar low. This strategy tries to capture what is nothing more than a short term pullup in a downtrend.

Source: © TradeStation Technologies, Inc. 1991–2005

Ericsson—Bull Fake Strategy

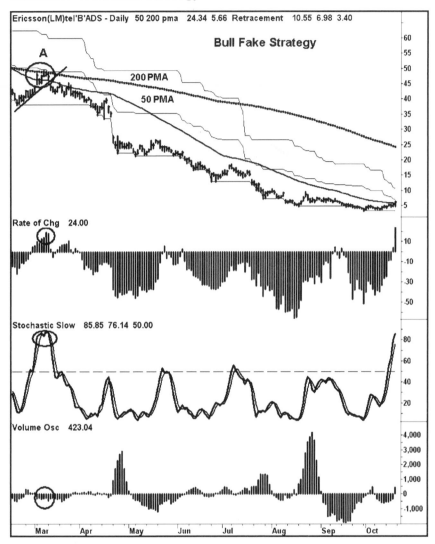

FIGURE 8.12 Bull Fake Strategy: Ericsson

The Bull Fake strategy on the daily ERICY chart meets all the criteria of this powerful setup. At point A price moves above the downward sloping 50 PMA with a declining 200 PMA. We then look for price moving below the downward sloping 50 PMA within one to six bars while moving below the low of the prior bar. This chart displays how stochastics alerted us to a move to the upper end of its recent range, indicating the pullup in a downtrend.

Source: © TradeStation Technologies, Inc. 1991–2005

THE END OF THE BEARISH PHASE

Part of our job as traders is to be vigilant to the end of trends that we are trading. The end of the Bearish Phase is characterized by several events, the first of which is the absence of new price lows being made over time. This is coupled with a flat-lined 60 period low channel indicator.

As traders and investors, we have to be prepared that some of our trades will not work out. Our approach is to accept the reality that some things will not work and prepare you so you can identify what that looks like. Being prepared, knowing what to look for if something is not working, will help you to act. Too many of the traders and investors we work with show up with no understanding of what to do when things go against them, and get paralyzed into inaction. This exacerbates losses. It is far better to realize, and be prepared, that some things will not work, and to look for the signs of a Bearish Phase failure, and have in your trading plan the action steps you will take if it materializes.

In a maturing Bearish Phase, particularly after a long downtrend, as time progresses, price begins to move sideways, often with a slight upward bias. If this is the case, the moving averages are going to catch up to price, either because price increases to them or because the averages decline to price. As this begins to unfold, prices will start to close above the downward sloping 50 moving average. The market begins to lose the strong momentum that characterizes the Bearish Phase, and our two momentum indicators will start to exhibit signs of strength.

Our Rate of Change indicator will not be declining sharply the way it was when prices originally declined. Our stochastics will start giving us higher readings, telling us that current and recent closes are at the upper end of the recent range. In a downtrending market, the first closes above the 50 period moving average may only signify pullups to the downward sloping 50 moving average. If prices quickly fall and start closing back below the 50 PMA, these short periods of tests of the 50 period moving average are Bull Fakes and are tradable. Time is frequently a factor in the failure of a Bearish Phase. This can materialize in several ways. One of these is that the lowest low channel starts to increase, signifying higher lows are materializing. Another can be that the higher channel starts to increase, signifying higher highs are appearing. As time marches on, price will start to consistently and consecutively close above the 50 period moving average, and that 50 period moving average will start pointing up. This leads us into the conditions for the Recovery Phase.

BEARISH PHASE FAILURE CHART

Bearish Phase failures are often a function of an exhausted, extensive bottoming process after a downtrend (see Figure 8.13 on the following page). Price has been moving sideways, not making new 60 period lows. If the price rallies back above the 50 PMA, this means the phase has failed. Selling pressure has subsided, suggesting that investors or traders have no more to sell. A Bearish Phase failure is more likely if the 200 PMA is flat or beginning to slope up, indicating that the long downtrend has lost its power. Under those conditions, there is likely to be little spread between the 50 PMA and the 200 PMA, which would be additional evidence that the phase may fail. The ROC may be positive, indicating an inability for price be below the preceding lows. Stochastics may be below 50, indicating that closes are in the lower region of the recent range, but they start rising. There is no need for volume on the rally because there is no one left to sell; prices can rise without much volume.

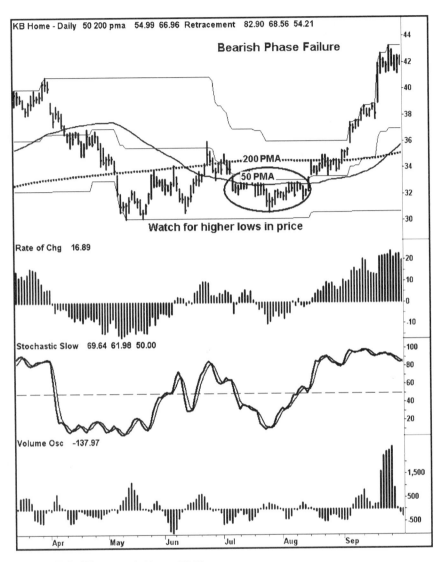

FIGURE 8.13 Bearish Phase: KB Home

The Bearish Phase failure chart of KBH provides us with several clues to the potential of a reversal back to the upside and thus a failure of the Bearish Phase. The upward sloping 200 PMA alerts us that the long term price structure is still sound. Additionally, there are no new lows, and there is light volume on the pushdown. No new lows are the best evidence that price trend has halted, which is not what a weaker Bearish Phase stock would show. Note that once price rallies back out of the Bearish Phase when leaving the right side of the circled area, it also crosses back above the 50 percent retracement line, and the 50 PMA starts sloping up. This suggests prices strengthening, not weakening.

Source: © TradeStation Technologies, Inc. 1991–2005

CHAPTER 9

Pulling It Together

In the preceding six chapters, we have examined each phase in detail. We can now pull all these concepts together with a discussion of how financial instruments cycle though the phases.

To summarize, the *TREND*advisor Diamond is broken into two equal and distinct sections, as shown in Figure 9.1. The left side of the *TREND*advisor Diamond is the "buy side" and the right side is the "sell side." There are six phases of price behavior in the Diamond: two clearly trending and four where the trend is less evident, where it could be ending or beginning. The two phases where there is sharpest price movement over time are the Bullish Phase for the uptrend and the Bearish Phase for the downtrend. If the market has exhibited an expansion of trend over time, the likelihood of a pullback should unfold. The Warning Phase in an uptrend and the Recovery Phase in a downtrend might be signaling the start of what could be the beginning of a countertrend move.

BUY SIDE PHASES

The groupings of the Recovery, Accumulation, and Bullish phases describe what we call the "buy side" phases (see Figure 9.2).

The progression of a chart from Recovery into Accumulation and then into the Bullish Phase shows how uptrends unfold. (Refer to Figure 9.3.) At Point A, note that price is in the Bearish Phase. However, we have several clues that this is a late stage Bearish Phase and susceptible to

FIGURE 9.1   The *TREND*advisor Diamond
The Diamond is broken into two equal and distinct sections. The left side of the Diamond is the "buy side" and the right side is the "sell side." Each side has three phases—the buy side includes the Recovery, Accumulation, and Bullish phases, and the sell side includes the Warning, Distribution, and Bearish Phases.

reversal. These clues include a flat 200 PMA, which indicates that the long term downtrend has lost its punch and a long basing pattern has been occurring; the 50 PMA and the 200 PMA are converging, again indicating the recent trend and long term trend are coming together. This indicates a state of equilibrium, a balance of supply and demand, when buyers and sellers are roughly equally matched. At point B, Allergan enters the Recovery Phase. Note that upon this entry, almost all the criteria for an ideal Recovery Phase chart are met (for more detail see Chapter 3 or the summary *TREND*advisor Diamond Matrix below), including price being above the 50 percent retracement line of the channel; a positive, rising Rate of Change; and stochastics rising and crossing above 50. At point C, the Accumulation Phase begins. Almost immediately, the higher highs that define an uptrend start. The slope of the 200 PMA transitions from down to up—these are all favorable characteristics we want to see in the phase. At D, the Bullish Phase begins. Volume surged on the recent breakout to new

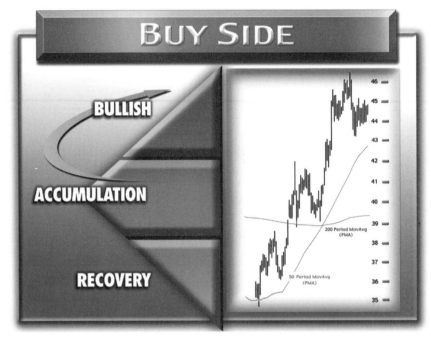

FIGURE 9.2 The Buy Side
The left side of the *TREND*advisor Diamond is the "buy side." It has three phases—
the Recovery, Accumulation, and Bullish phases—which describe the progression
of prices in an uptrend.

highs, and has contracted on the consolidation that is happening when D
appears.

How might *TREND*advisor trade this using the tactics we discussed in
the individual chapters? Remember, this is a description of our methodology, based on our objectives that are short term in nature. You must develop your own trading plan and objectives, and create methodologies
that are compatible with those. Using the guidelines we detailed in the individual chapters, here is one way we might approach trading this chart.

Assume we have no open positions prior to point B. At point B, we
would initiate a new long position, using one-third of the capital of a normal sized position, determined by how diversified our portfolio must be
(see the discussion in each of the phase chapters regarding this). Let's assume, for the sake of this example, that a normal, full position size in our
well diversified portfolio with this stock translates into 600 shares. We use
one-third of a normal position size because there are risks to this phase.
At point B, we purchase 200 shares. Our initial stop could be a close back

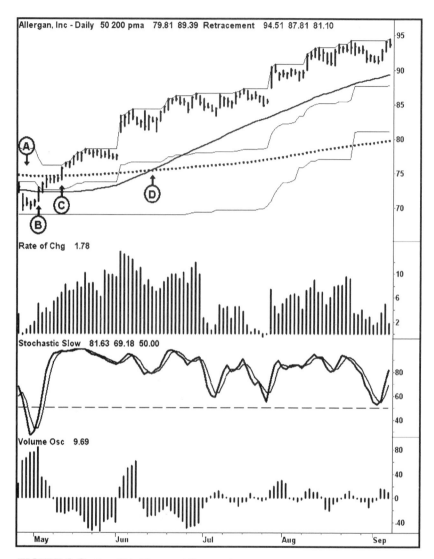

FIGURE 9.3 Buy Side Phases: Allergan, Inc.

From the Bearish Phase at point A, Allergan enters the Recovery Phase at point B. Note that during the Recovery Phase (between points B and C), AGN starts closing in the top half of the narrowing channel. At point C, it enters the Accumulation Phase. Immediately, it starts making the higher highs that define an uptrend. Note also that the 200 PMA has been flat, indicating a long consolidation preceding this, and that the 200 PMA transitions from down slope to up slope, kicking the longer term trend from down to up. At point D, AGN enters the Bullish Phase, triggered by the 50 PMA crossing above the 200 PMA. The uptrend continues to unfold with higher highs and shallow pullbacks on low volume.

Source: © TradeStation Technologies, Inc. 1991–2005

below the 50 PMA, which would constitute a phase failure. Given the narrowing channel, we might choose 5 percent as our initial profit target, where we will harvest part of our trade. At point C, two things happen. First, we have hit our initial profit target. This means we sell 100 shares of our first position, and we increase the stop on the remaining shares to the entry price of that position (be sure you understand how to manage stop orders, and work with a broker who is well skilled in this).

Next, we enter a new phase. In the Accumulation Phase, we can be long up to two-thirds of a normal position size. This means we buy an additional 200 shares, giving us a total of 300 shares (we recognize this is not two-thirds of 600 shares, but we are trying to illustrate our concept of money management and harvesting profits). The stop on the new 200 shares is placed at a close below the 200 PMA, which would constitute a phase failure. Again, our profit target for harvesting part of our trade on the second position is 5 percent. Some time early in June, when the stock gaps up, this profit target is hit. We harvest 100 shares and raise our stop on the remaining shares to the entry price of the second position (the price at point C). We now have only 200 shares total, which is less than we could have, but we have booked two profits, which is consistent with our objectives and methodology of continuously harvesting profits.

Along comes the entry in the Bullish Phase at point D. We can have on a full position here a total of 600 shares, but our current position is only 200 shares. Therefore, we purchase an additional 400 shares at point D. Our initial stop is a close below the 50 PMA, which would constitute a phase failure. Our profit target for harvesting part of the trade increases to 10 percent. This is for two reasons. The first is that the evidence of an uptrend is firmly in place—we have better chances for a rally. The second is that price range has expanded; there is a greater range than at B or C so a greater objective is warranted. So at point D we have a full 600 share position.

As prices rise, we continue to raise our stop with the rising 50 PMA. Sometime in August, our 10 percent objective is hit. We harvest half the position, 300 shares, and raise our stop to the greater of entry price or the 50 PMA. As time goes by, we continue to increase our stop on the remaining 300 shares to the 50 PMA. Eventually, this rising stop will get hit, and we will harvest the rest of the trade.

This is not the only way to trade this chart. Long-only portfolio managers could enter a new position, underweight the benchmark at point B, and go to overweight at C and D. More active traders (to complement the description of our methodology above) could trade back into the harvested profits on the pullbacks once the trend is clearly established, using the drops in either the ROC or stochastics indicators to guide the entry. The point is this: have a consistent methodology you deploy, one that is in alignment with your objectives.

THE *TREND*advisor DIAMOND MATRIX—BUY SIDE

Buy Side	**Recovery Phase**
50 PMA	Flat to sloping up
200 PMA	Sloping down
50% retracement	Price at or above
60 period higher highs	Not required
60 period higher lows	Not required
Rate of Change (ROC)	Begins to turn positive
Stochastic	Starts to climb above the 50 zone
Volume oscillator	Starts to climb above the zero line

Buy Side	**Accumulation Phase**
50 PMA	Sloping up
200 PMA	Sideways with up bias
50% retracement	Price above
60 period higher highs	Price making new 60 period higher highs
60 period higher lows	We begin to see 60 period higher lows
Rate of Change (ROC)	In positive territory
Stochastic	Is above the 50 zone
Volume oscillator	Above zero on price expansion

Buy Side	**Bullish Phase**
50 PMA	Sloping up
200 PMA	Sloping up
50% retracement	Price above
60 period higher highs	Price making new 60 period higher highs
60 period higher lows	Channel making 60 period higher lows
Rate of Change (ROC)	In positive territory
Stochastic	Is above the 50 zone
Volume oscillator	Above zero on price expansion

SELL SIDE PHASES

The groupings of Warning, Distribution, and Bearish phases describe what we call the sell side phases. (See Figure 9.4.) Sell side includes exiting long as well as entering short.

The progression of a chart from Warning into Distribution and then into the Bearish Phase shows how downtrends unfold. (Refer to Figure 9.5.) At point A, price enters the Warning Phase. There are several clues of a tired uptrend preceding this, which makes the financial instrument susceptible

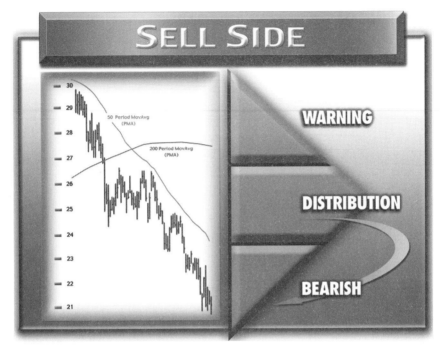

FIGURE 9.4   The Sell Side
The right side of the *TREND*advisor Diamond is the "sell side."   It has three phases—the Warning, Distribution, and Bearish phases—which describe the progression of prices in a downtrend.

to reversal. These clues include a flat 200 PMA, which indicates that the long term uptrend has lost its punch and a long topping pattern has been occurring; the 50 PMA and the 200 PMA are close together; again indicating that the recent trend and long term trend are coming together. This indicates a state of equilibrium, a balance of supply and demand; buyers and sellers are roughly equally matched. However, at point A, price is still in the upper half of the channel, above the 50 percent retracement line. This is not ideal. However, shortly thereafter, before point B, price starts closing below that 50 percent retracement level in the lower half of the channel. This produces more evidence of weakening, along with ROC going negative and the precipitous drop in stochastics. At point B, Avaya enters the Distribution Phase. Note that upon this entry, almost all the criteria for an ideal Distribution Phase chart are met (see Chapter 7 for more detail or the summary *TREND*advisor Diamond Matrix below), including punching into a new low in the 60 period high/low channel, price being below the 50

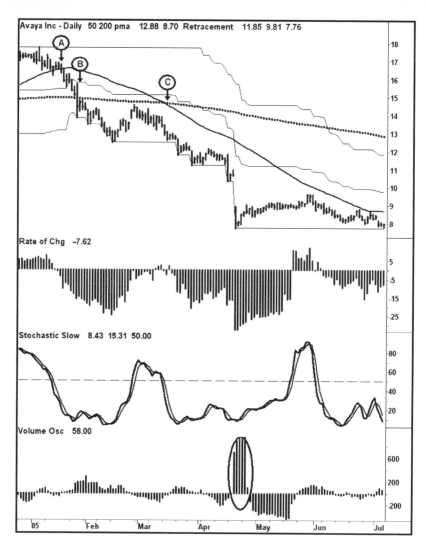

FIGURE 9.5 Sell Side Phases: Avaya, Inc.

Preceding point A, Avaya had been going sideways for some time, as seen in the flat 200 PMA. Note that shortly before point A, price failed on a weak rally to the 60 period high channel. This is common in late stage, maturing Bullish Phase charts. At point A, AV enters the Warning Phase with closes below the 50 PMA. Heading into point B, price starts closing below the 50 percent retracement line of the 60 period high/low channel, a sign of weakening. At point B, AV closes below the 200 PMA, entering the Distribution Phase. The 200 PMA has transitioned from up slope to down slope, and when entering the phase at point B, a new low appears in the 60 period high/low channel, which is the start of the downtrend. Note that volume has been increasing. At Point C, the 50 PMA crosses below the 200 PMA, triggering the Bearish Phase. Finally, at the right side of the chart, note the long basing pattern—no new lows, the 50 PMA flattening, and the channel contracting. This is typical of mature Bearish Phase stocks, and visually captures the dynamic of "no more sellers" that we discussed in Chapter 1.

Source: © TradeStation Technologies, Inc. 1991–2005

178

percent retracement line of the channel, a negative, falling Rate of Change, and stochastics persistently low. Additionally, the slope of the 200 PMA transitions from up to down—these are all favorable characteristics we want to see in the phase. At point C, the Bearish Phase begins. Almost immediately, the lower lows that define a downtrend continue.

How might *TREND*advisor trade this using the tactics we discussed in the individual chapters? Remember, this is a description of our methodology, based on our objectives that are short term in nature. You must develop your own trading plan and objectives, and create methodologies that are compatible with those. Using the guidelines we detailed in the individual chapters, here is one way we might approach trading this chart. Assume we are long the stock going into point A. At point A, we would exit out of our long position. We would not enter a new short position immediately, because price is still in the upper half of the price channel, above the 50 percent retracement line of the 60 period high/low channel, thus violating one of our important criteria for an ideal setup. At point B, we would initiate a new short position, because the evidence of weakness that we detailed above is appearing. This entry into the Distribution Phase means we can deploy two-thirds of the capital of a normal sized short position. Let's assume, for the sake of this example, a normal, full position size in our well diversified portfolio with this stock translates into 600 shares. We use two-thirds of a normal position size because there are risks to this phase.

At point B, we sell short 400 shares. Our initial stop could be a close back above the 200 PMA, which would constitute a phase failure. Given the expanding channel, we might choose 10 percent as our initial profit target, where we will harvest part of our trade. Long before point C, about 15 bars after point B, we hit our initial profit target. This means we buy to cover one-half of our short position, or 200 shares, leaving us short 200 shares. We decrease the stop on the remaining shares to the entry price of that position (be sure you understand how to manage stop orders and work with a broker who is well skilled in this). Next, on that rally about half way between point B and point C, this lowered stop at our entry price will trigger and we will cover the remaining shares at breakeven. One profit, one breakeven—this is the kind of thing that happens when trading!

At point C, this instrument enters the Bearish Phase. We can have a full short position here of a total of 600 shares, but our current position is 0 shares. Therefore, we short 600 shares at point C. Our initial stop is a close above the 50 PMA, which would constitute a phase failure. Our profit target for harvesting part of the trade increases to 20 percent. This is for several reasons. The first is that the evidence of a downtrend is firmly in place—we have better chances for more selling. The second is that price range has expanded; there is a greater range than at B so a greater objective is warranted. Finally, this is a lower priced stock—

higher percentages are more likely in lower priced stocks. So at point C, we are short a full 600 share position. As prices fall, we continue to lower our stop with the declining 50 PMA. Some time in April, probably on that large gap down, our 20 percent objective is hit. We harvest half the position, 300 shares, and lower our stop to the lesser of entry price or the 50 PMA. As time goes by, we continue to decrease our stop on the remaining 300 shares to the 50 PMA. Eventually, this lowering stop will get hit, and we will harvest the rest of the trade by covering the remaining short.

THE *TREND*advisor DIAMOND MATRIX—SELL SIDE

Sell Side	**Warning Phase**
50 PMA	Flat to sloping down
200 PMA	Sloping up
50% retracement	At or below
60 period lower highs	Not required
60 period lower lows	Not required
Rate of Change (ROC)	Begins to turn negative
Stochastic	Starts its move below the 50 zone
Volume oscillator	Above zero on the selloffs

Sell Side	**Distribution Phase**
50 PMA	Sloping down
200 PMA	Sideways with downward bias
50% retracement	Price below
60 period lower highs	We begin to see 60 period lower highs
60 period lower lows	Price making new 60 period lower lows
Rate of Change (ROC)	In negative territory
Stochastic	Is below the 50 zone
Volume oscillator	Above zero on the selloffs

Sell Side	**Bearish Phase**
50 PMA	Sloping down
200 PMA	Sloping down
50% retracement	Price below
60 period lower highs	Price making new 60 period lower highs
60 period lower lows	Channel making 60 period lower lows
Rate of Change (ROC)	In negative territory
Stochastic	Is below the 50 zone
Volume oscillator	Above zero on the selloffs

This is not the only way to trade this chart. For example, if the stop on the position shorted at point B remained a close above the 200 PMA instead of our lowering it to entry price after harvesting at the first objective, one would not have been stopped out. This would have led to an additional, profitable position (however, it would have violated our methodology so we didn't describe it. Of all things in trading, discipline is paramount—see Chapter 10). To complement the description of our methodology above, more active traders could re-short the harvested positions on the pushup rallies once the downtrend is clearly established, using the rises in either the ROC or stochastics indicators to guide the entry. A long-only portfolio manager could reduce from overweight to neutral at point A, go to underweight the position against the benchmark at B, and avoid it altogether at C. The point is this: have a consistent methodology you deploy, one that is in alignment with your objectives.

SUMMARY

In Figure 9.6 we have an example of a financial instrument cycling through all six phases. At point A, Janus Capital Group enters the Warning Phase. The price is still above the 50 percent retracement line of the 60 period high/low channel, but the ROC has gone negative and stochastics drop below 50. At point B, things are much more negative, with the price pushing into the 60 period low channel; the slope of the 50 PMA down; the slope of the 200 PMA down; and volume increasing on the selloff. At point C, the Bearish Phase is triggered. Note that the weak rally just prior to point C failed at the downward sloping 200 PMA. At point D, price closes back above the 50 PMA, thus triggering the Recovery Phase. It is also closing above the 50 percent retracement line of the 60 period high/low channel. ROC goes positive, stochastics are above 50, and there is a nice surge of volume on the rally. At point E, this financial instrument goes into the Accumulation Phase, again with positive characteristics. At point F, it enters the Bullish Phase. You can quiz yourself about this Bullish Phase—given what you have learned, is it a high quality Bullish Phase chart or is it more suspect? (See the *TREND*advisor buy side summary matrix earlier in the chapter, if you need clues.)

Warning! The World Is Not This Picture Perfect!

We have included examples to train your eye for what high quality setups look like. This could imply that all setups and charts look as picture perfect as the charts we have included. We can assure you that this

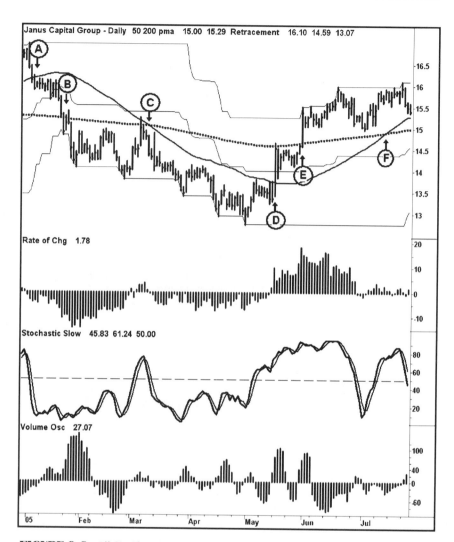

FIGURE 9.6 All Six Phases: Janus Capital Group
This chart shows the progression of a financial instrument through all six phases.
Janus Captital Group enters the Warning Phase at point A, transitions into the Distribution Phase at point B, crosses into the Bearish Phase at point C, starts the Recovery Phase at point D, enters the Accumulation Phase at point E, and progresses into the Bullish Phase at point F.
Source: © TradeStation Technologies, Inc. 1991–2005

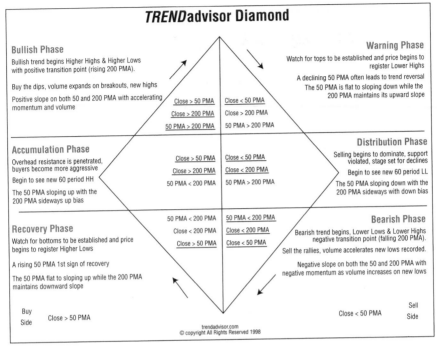

FIGURE 9.7 The *TREND*advisor Diamond with Phase Definitions
This figure summarizes the relationships of price closes and the moving averages, which define the phases. It also shows the progression of the price cycles through the phases.

is not the case—the real world of trading includes much more ambiguity than is implied by the clarity of our examples. You will encounter much murkiness when you try to put these principles to work in your trading or investing (see Figure 9.7).

That said, we can also reassure you that there is always something in a clearly defined trend. Our web site, www.trendadvisor.com, seeks out and exploits the opportunities that appear each day in the markets. You are welcome to contact us there if we can answer your questions or assist you on your way.

CHAPTER 10

Discipline and Money Management Come from Your Trading Plan

In trading or investing there is usually too much emphasis placed on indicators and setups and too little attention toward the issues of discipline and money management. Based on our many years of experience in teaching, coaching, and mentoring hundreds of traders, we have identified the factors that lead to success as well as those that lead to failure. The factors fall into three distinct areas:

- **Discipline:** 50 percent of the success model
- **Business trading plan:** 30 percent of the success model
- **Technical/fundamental analysis:** 20 percent of the success model

Many traders want the sizzle of the latest and greatest indicator, but what they most need is to be firmly rooted in the crucial areas of discipline and a plan. Of the top ten cardinal mistakes traders make, lack of discipline and lack of a money management process rate one and two. Disciplined traders always operate from a position of strength, consistently deploying their methodology and plan into the markets, using appropriate, defined capital allocation in their trading, which is designed to reduce risk while allowing for reward. They harvest their profits and take their losses according to their plan. They trade what they see—not what they think or feel.

A well defined plan increases your chances for success for several reasons. The first is that it prepares you, and gives you a plan, for how to deal with losses. The number one mistake we see in the investors and traders who come to us is that they have no plan for how to take losses (and harvest profits). Some statistically significant number of your investments or trades will not work. Given this fact, what must happen is that you must keep losses as small as realistically possible. Too often, there is either no exit strategy or no stop in the market. When a long trade sells off, and drops below the level where it should be stopped out, an elaborate wish fulfillment process happens, and while prices keep dropping, and losses mounting, more and more wishful thinking happens. Eventually, the losses and pressure become so severe that the position is finally exited (we call it "puking" the trade because it has both the messiness and the relief of that physical event). This is the classic example of feelings dictating the trade— the feelings are so bad, and the pressure so great, that they become what causes the exit, not a well defined plan.

A trading plan helps you to define the amount of money that will be lost in the trade if the stop price is triggered. Next, a good trading plan will help you to define when and how you will take profits. Too many investors and traders "let it ride," in which case what were once profitable positions turn into losses because there never was a strategy for how to capture those profits. A trading plan will help you to define entry and exits. Once defined, orders can be in the market to trigger at the appropriate prices, which is one way of assuring discipline.

Your trading plan should incorporate all the following elements:

- Your objectives. This should include what you are going to accomplish from your trading or investing.
- What markets and time frames you are going to trade. Generally, time means risk but also reward. The longer your time frame, the greater the risk and thus the reward. The shorter the time frame, the more active you will have to be.
- What markets or instruments you are going to trade. The higher the risk, the more should be the reward. Trading illiquid, smaller stocks or highly leveraged commodities means you are taking on more risk and your reward could be higher.
- What is the maximum number of positions you will carry? This is to help you determine how much of your capital you put in any one trade. Generally, the more diversified you are, the lower the risk. You do not need to have all your money at work all the time. If you cannot find acceptable trades or investments that meet your rules, it should be acceptable to you to be in cash with those parts of your capital that you can't find trades for. However, the more diversified across positions you are, the more time and attention you will require to manage your trading. You need to define what balances these different issues for you.
- You also need to determine how much of your capital you are willing to lose in any one position before exiting it. This is your absolute stop.
- You must define how you will deploy capital in your trading. You should also determine how full a position size you will put on in a spe-

cific phase. For example, "I will have only one-third of my normal position size on in the Recovery Phase." There are a variety of ways that the *TREND*advisor Diamond Analysis Money Management Model can be utilized in capital deployment. One way is to have full long positions only in instruments that are in the Bullish Phase, and full short positions only in instruments in the Bearish Phase, while having less capital exposed in the other phases. For example, a full long position in the Bullish Phase could be logically reduced when the instrument passes from Bullish into Warning, and eliminated or further reduced if the instrument transitions into the Distribution Phase (however, the longer the time to exit, and the more deterioration there is in the price, the less profit there will be or the greater the losses will be). From the short perspective, a full short position could be in the Bearish Phase, and reduced or eliminated on transitions into the Recovery or Accumulation Phases. On the flip side, when interested in going long, a lesser initial position could be entered in the Recovery or Accumulation Phases, increasing exposure as prices transition into the stronger price phases.

The example above deploys full positions in the safety and strength of either a Bullish or Bearish Phase. Another approach could be laddering your position based on the strength of the phase. An investor might choose to build a long term position in a financial instrument. The phase analysis money management model would then look like this: in the Recovery Phase where price begins to build its base, we would expose a one-third position. As price begins to stabilize or improve and makes its move to the Accumulation Phase, we would increase exposure by another one-third position. We now have a two-thirds position at risk. As price cycles to the Bullish Phase where safety and strength are at their optimum, another one-third position is added, bringing the exposure to a full position. These are just examples. The point is that you must define how you will deploy your capital.

- You also need to define your rules for entry, rules for exit, where your stops are to be placed, and what your profit taking rules are. For example, you could decide that for any position you are in, if it is profitable by 10 percent, you will harvest half the position, raise your stop to the entry price on the remainder, and exit the remainder if it is up xx percent or when the phase fails.

- Periodically, you need to evaluate your system. This can be done on a regular schedule or it can be done if you go into a losing streak. You need to define what constitutes failure. When you are in a losing streak, is it that you have abandoned your methodology, or has the market changed and you are fighting it? How frequently will you update your methodology?

- Resources—Where will your ideas come from? What charting services will you use for your screening and analysis? What brokerage firm for your executions? These decisions need to balance cost, effectiveness, and support. From our charts, you can see that we use TradeStation (www.tradestation.com). It is a comprehensive program that allows us to customize our indicators, to screen automatically for things that meet our conditions in real time, and automate our executions. Also, TradeStation has a brokerage firm that is price competitive with other discount brokers, which gives us a one-stop solution. We also use Telecharts (www.worden.com), which is quite cost effective, has easy scanning, good speed for sorting through a great number of issues, allows screening on fundamental criteria, and has programming capability for customizing tools.
- Using mentoring or trading coaches. When training to become a doctor, medical students work side-by-side with experienced professionals who can guide them to success and steer them away from errors. Should you do the same? We find that even highly experienced portfolio managers and professional traders work with mentors and coaches—it helps to collaborate in making decisions.

Discipline in trading means acting on your plan when the criteria are met. In order to have discipline, you must have a plan. If you have a plan and no discipline, your success, if any, will be from random factors or pure luck. If you have discipline and no plan, you will not know what to be doing or when to be doing it. Finally, if you do not use appropriate money management, you risk losing your capital, without which you cannot trade or invest.

So as a wise trader once advised us, and we pass along to you: "Plan your trade, trade your plan, use stops, and manage your capital appropriately!"

CHAPTER 11

A Lens on
the Past

Because we can be precise about what defines each phase, it is possible to categorize market behavior into our six specific phases. For example, in the last 20 years the S&P 500 has spent 53 percent of the time in the Bullish Phase, 17 percent in the Warning Phase, and 14 percent in the Bearish Phase. But in the last five years the market has spent 32 percent of the time in the Bearish Phase, 28 percent of the time in the Bullish Phase, and 16 percent of the time in the Recovery Phase.

Phase definition allows the quantification of strength, and allows comparisons between financial instruments. For example, if an index has predominantly Bullish characteristics, but a stock in that index is less so, we know that that stock is relatively weak and may not be considered as a trading candidate. However, if a stock has stronger characteristics than the index, it may be outperforming the index and thus a good candidate for trading. If Crude Oil is exhibiting Bullish characteristics and the bond market is not, long-only portfolio managers could seek new long ideas in the crude sector, and avoid financials that trade like bonds.

STATISTICAL ANALYSIS

With the precision of phase definition, we can statistically analyze market strength and or weakness. What follows are four tables of daily price data: 1 year, 10 years, 20 years, and 75 years. These tables summarize the percentage of time the tradable financial instrument's price occupies each phase. All tables are sorted with the Bullish Phase at the top of each table. On the buy side, when price occupies the Bullish Phase, a 60 period channel higher high is accumulated *only in that phase*. On the sell side, when price is in the Bearish Phase, each new 60 period channel lower low accumulates *only in that phase*. The tables are divided into the *buy side phases* and the *sell side phases*.

As an example, Table 11.1 shows how over the past year the Dow Jones Transportation Average (line 1) occupied the Bullish Phase 77 percent of the time; while in that phase, price accumulated 36 new 60 period channel higher highs. During that same time period, price resided in the Bearish Phase 0 percent of the time while making 0 new 60 period channel lower lows.

In Table 11.2 we reference the Dow Jones Industrial Average of 19,000 daily bars, making up 75 years of price activity. Price occupied the Bullish Phase 44 percent of the time, while in that phase, price accumulated 1833 new 60 period channel higher highs. During that same time period, price resided in the Bearish Phase 19 percent of the time while making 507 new

TABLE 11.1   One Year, 8/03–8/04

	Symbol	Description	1 Buy Side Phase %				1 Sell Side Phase %			
			Recovery	Accumulation	Bullish	60 Period HH	Warning	Distribution	Bearish	60 Period LL
1	$TRAN	Dow Jones Transportation	0%	0%	77%	36	17%	6%	0%	0
2	$DJU	Dow Jones Utilities Index	0%	0%	71%	32	29%	0%	0%	0
3	$INX	S&P 500 Index	0%	0%	69%	39	26%	5%	0%	0
4	$INDU	Dow Jones Industrial Aver	0%	0%	69%	42	22%	7%	2%	0
5	$COMPX	Nasdaq Composite Index	0%	4%	61%	38	22%	6%	8%	3
6	Dow Jones Industrial Avg (30)									
7	PG	Procter & Gamble	0%	0%	85%	43	11%	4%	0%	0
8	XOM	Exxon Mobil	0%	0%	82%	46	13%	5%	0%	0
9	BA	Boeing Co	0%	0%	79%	33	21%	0%	0%	0
10	MMM	3M Co	0%	0%	76%	37	23%	1%	0%	0
11	HON	Honeywell Intl	0%	0%	73%	31	27%	0%	0%	0
12	MCD	McDonald's Corp	0%	0%	70%	28	27%	3%	0%	0
13	$INDU	Dow Jones Industrial Aver	0%	0%	69%	42	22%	7%	2%	0
14	DIS	Disney (Walt) Co	0%	0%	64%	18	24%	12%	0%	0
15	AXP	Amer Express	0%	0%	62%	23	33%	5%	0%	0
16	KO	Coca-Cola Co	0%	0%	58%	18	34%	8%	0%	0
17	MO	Altria Group	0%	0%	57%	32	21%	12%	11%	0
18	UTX	United Technologies	0%	15%	56%	31	19%	5%	4%	2
19	CAT	Caterpillar Inc	2%	5%	56%	26	23%	11%	4%	1
20	GM	General Motors	0%	4%	55%	21	24%	7%	9%	2
21	GE	General Electric	0%	5%	55%	23	31%	8%	2%	0
22	AA	Alcoa Inc	10%	0%	54%	32	19%	7%	9%	0
23	C	Citigroup Inc	0%	0%	51%	20	25%	10%	14%	5
24	JPM	JPMorgan Chase & Co	3%	3%	51%	23	27%	9%	7%	0
25	AIG	Amer Intl Group	0%	0%	50%	31	48%	2%	0%	0
26	HD	Home Depot	2%	1%	49%	15	33%	5%	10%	0
27	IBM	Intl Bus. Machines	5%	0%	45%	19	21%	13%	16%	4
28	DD	Dupont(E.I.)DeNemours	1%	9%	43%	4	10%	31%	6%	0
29	INTC	Intel Corp	13%	0%	40%	22	19%	8%	20%	9
30	HPQ	Hewlett-Packard	4%	0%	37%	11	30%	9%	19%	3
31	MSFT	Microsoft Corp	12%	11%	37%	10	11%	20%	10%	2
32	PFE	Pfizer, Inc	3%	9%	33%	16	28%	16%	11%	1
33	JNJ	Johnson & Johnson	16%	7%	32%	10	7%	7%	30%	7
34	WMT	Wal-Mart Stores	3%	11%	31%	9	15%	19%	21%	7
35	SBC	SBC Communications	5%	15%	21%	8	17%	24%	19%	12
36	VZ	Verizon Communications	9%	13%	14%	3	22%	15%	28%	6
37	MRK	Merck & Co	31%	7%	3%	1	2%	19%	38%	18

| ◄ | ◄ | ► | ►| | 75 Years 8/29 - 8/04 | 20 Years 8/84 - 8/04 | 10 Years 8/94 - 8/04 | 5 Years 8/99 - 8/04 | 3 Years 8/01 - 8/04 | 1 Year 8/03 - 8/04 |

TABLE 11.2 Seventy-Five Years, 8/29–8/04

	Symbol	Description	1 Buy Side Phase %				1 Sell Side Phase %			
			Recovery	Accumulation	Bullish	60 Period HH	Warning	Distribution	Bearish	60 Period LL
1	$INDU	Dow Jones Industrial Aver	9%	6%	44%	1,833	15%	6%	19%	507
2										

75 Years 8/29 - 8/04 \ 20 Years 8/84 - 8/04 \ 10 Years 8/94 - 8/04 \ 5 Years 8/99 - 8/04 \ 3 Years 8/01 - 8/04 \ 1 Year 8/03 - 8/04

60 period channel lower lows. The table illustrates 63 percent of all price activity occupying either the Bullish or Bearish Phases.

COMPARATIVE ANALYSIS

Now that precise definitions of phases have been outlined and analyzed statistically, various financial instruments can be compared using this data. For the comparative examples, the Dow Jones Industrial Average equities are ranked according to a top-down approach to phase strength and weakness over a 10-year span. See Table 11.3. In Table 11.4, a 20-year view of the strongest index is compared to the weakest equity.

TABLE 11.3 Ten Years, 8/94–8/04

	Symbol	Description	1 Buy Side Phase %				1 Sell Side Phase %			
			Recovery	Accumulation	Bullish	60 Period HH	Warning	Distribution	Bearish	60 Period LL
1	$INX	S&P 500 Index	9%	4%	52%	335	14%	5%	17%	66
2	$INDU	Dow Jones Industrial Aver	7%	8%	49%	297	14%	8%	13%	48
3	$COMPX	Nasdaq Composite Index	7%	6%	49%	364	13%	5%	20%	96
4	$DJU	Dow Jones Utilities Index	11%	6%	43%	211	15%	5%	20%	51
5	$TRAN	Dow Jones Transportation	11%	8%	42%	194	14%	7%	18%	77
6	Dow Jones Industrial Avg (30)									
7	PG	Procter & Gamble	5%	6%	56%	240	19%	6%	8%	17
8	JNJ	Johnson & Johnson	6%	6%	54%	225	18%	6%	10%	36
9	AXP	Amer Express	7%	7%	51%	189	18%	6%	11%	30
10	GE	General Electric	7%	4%	50%	234	17%	3%	18%	50
11	$INDU	Dow Jones Industrial Aver	7%	8%	49%	297	14%	8%	13%	48
12	AIG	Amer Intl Group	7%	5%	49%	219	19%	6%	14%	43
13	UTX	United Technologies	8%	9%	48%	217	15%	5%	14%	47
14	XOM	Exxon Mobil	8%	8%	48%	178	16%	9%	11%	18
15	PFE	Pfizer, Inc	7%	8%	48%	201	14%	6%	18%	50
16	MSFT	Microsoft Corp	7%	7%	46%	213	18%	7%	14%	45
17	MMM	3M Co	7%	7%	46%	151	20%	10%	10%	30
18	HD	Home Depot	8%	6%	44%	191	17%	6%	18%	40
19	MRK	Merck & Co	10%	6%	43%	194	14%	8%	18%	60
20	IBM	Intl Bus. Machines	4%	9%	43%	214	21%	8%	15%	38
21	MO	Altria Group	8%	9%	42%	205	15%	8%	19%	45
22	KO	Coca-Cola Co	10%	8%	41%	186	15%	8%	19%	66
23	HPQ	Hewlett-Packard	8%	6%	41%	150	16%	7%	22%	64
24	INTC	Intel Corp	10%	6%	41%	230	15%	5%	22%	70
25	WMT	Wal-Mart Stores	8%	9%	40%	172	15%	8%	19%	49
26	BA	Boeing Co	11%	6%	40%	132	16%	6%	21%	67
27	HON	Honeywell Intl	11%	8%	40%	153	17%	5%	19%	46
28	JPM	JPMorgan Chase & Co	10%	9%	40%	193	14%	9%	18%	53
29	DIS	Disney (Walt) Co	12%	5%	39%	126	15%	6%	22%	79
30	AA	Alcoa Inc	9%	9%	39%	144	19%	7%	18%	54
31	CAT	Caterpillar Inc	10%	8%	38%	137	16%	9%	18%	58
32	MCD	McDonald's Corp	12%	8%	37%	156	12%	7%	24%	86
33	VZ	Verizon Communications	10%	8%	35%	114	15%	10%	23%	62
34	DD	Dupont(E.I.)DeNemours	11%	9%	33%	94	15%	10%	22%	55
35	GM	General Motors	15%	7%	32%	101	15%	8%	22%	61
36	SBC	SBC Communications	12%	8%	32%	135	14%	7%	27%	73

75 Years 8/29 - 8/04 \ 20 Years 8/84 - 8/04 \ 10 Years 8/94 - 8/04 \ 5 Years 8/99 - 8/04 \ 3 Years 8/01 - 8/04 \ 1 Year 8/03 - 8/04

TABLE 11.4 Twenty Years, 8/84–8/04

	Symbol	Description	1 Buy Side Phase %				1 Sell Side Phase %			
			Recovery	Accumulation	Bullish	60 Period HH	Warning	Distribution	Bearish	60 Period LL
1	$INX	S&P 500 Index	8%	4%	55%	617	17%	5%	12%	77
2	$INDU	Dow Jones Industrial Aver	6%	7%	53%	598	16%	7%	11%	59
3	$COMPX	Nasdaq Composite Index	9%	6%	48%	702	15%	6%	16%	122
4	$TRAN	Dow Jones Transportation	10%	6%	46%	456	16%	6%	16%	103
5	$DJU	Dow Jones Utilities Index	10%	5%	42%	419	16%	6%	21%	118
6	Dow Jones Industrial Avg (30)									
7	$INDU	Dow Jones Industrial Aver	6%	7%	53%	598	16%	7%	11%	59
8	PG	Procter & Gamble	6%	7%	52%	407	18%	7%	10%	35
9	JNJ	Johnson & Johnson	8%	5%	52%	455	19%	5%	11%	68
10	KO	Coca-Cola Co	8%	6%	50%	448	16%	6%	14%	76
11	GE	General Electric	6%	6%	49%	412	18%	4%	16%	80
12	WMT	Wal-Mart Stores	7%	6%	49%	414	18%	7%	13%	61
13	AIG	Amer Intl Group	8%	6%	48%	426	17%	6%	15%	71
14	XOM	Exxon Mobil	6%	9%	48%	334	18%	9%	10%	33
15	MRK	Merck & Co	10%	4%	47%	457	14%	7%	17%	96
16	MO	Altria Group	7%	7%	47%	429	16%	7%	17%	85
17	MMM	3M Co	8%	7%	46%	315	18%	10%	11%	53
18	PFE	Pfizer, Inc	8%	8%	46%	375	15%	7%	16%	77
19	MCD	McDonald's Corp	9%	6%	45%	371	18%	6%	16%	91
20	AXP	Amer Express	9%	8%	44%	328	16%	6%	16%	73
21	DIS	Disney (Walt) Co	10%	8%	43%	317	15%	7%	17%	94
22	UTX	United Technologies	10%	9%	43%	328	17%	6%	15%	80
23	BA	Boeing Co	10%	6%	41%	314	17%	7%	19%	101
24	DD	Dupont(E.I.)DeNemours	10%	9%	39%	264	15%	9%	19%	82
25	CAT	Caterpillar Inc	10%	10%	38%	282	15%	9%	18%	104
26	JPM	JPMorgan Chase & Co	11%	9%	37%	288	14%	8%	22%	118
27	AA	Alcoa Inc	12%	9%	35%	257	16%	8%	20%	99
28	HPQ	Hewlett-Packard	10%	9%	35%	243	15%	8%	22%	125
29	IBM	Intl Bus. Machines	10%	9%	34%	323	16%	8%	23%	127
30	GM	General Motors	15%	8%	33%	225	17%	8%	20%	116

| | 75 Years 8/29 - 8/04 | 20 Years 8/84 - 8/04 | 10 Years 8/94 - 8/04 | 5 Years 8/99 - 8/04 | 3 Years 8/01 - 8/04 | 1 Year 8/03 - 8/04 |

Looking at line 7 over the past 10 years in Table 11.3, Procter & Gamble (P&G) had the greatest "safety" based on Bullish/Bearish Phase comparison. P&G occupied the Bullish Phase 56 percent of the time, accumulating 240 new 60 period channel higher highs. During that same time period, P&G's price resided in the Bearish Phase 8 percent of the time while making 17 new 60 period channel lower lows. Viewing the same 10-year period, SBC Communications had spent the least amount of time in the Bullish Phase, 32 percent, while accumulating 135 new 60 period channel higher highs. During that same 10-year time frame, SBC's price resided in the Bearish Phase 27 percent of the time while making 73 new 60 period channel lower lows.

Table 11.4 compares the strongest Bullish Phase index to the weakest Bearish Phase equity in the Dow Jones Industrial Average. The S&P 500 (line 1) had the greatest safety and strength, while IBM (line 29) lagged the overall market. The S&P 500 occupied the Bullish Phase 55 percent of the time, and while in that phase accumulated 617 new 60 period channel higher highs. During the same 20-year time span, IBM's price resided in the Bearish Phase 13 percent of the time, making 81 new 60 period channel lower lows. IBM occupied the Bullish Phase 34 percent of the time, accumulating 323 new 60 period channel higher highs. During that same 20 years, IBM's price resided in the Bearish Phase 23 percent of the time, making 130 new 60 period channel lower lows.

Drilling this comparative analysis one step further, the S&P 500 occupied the Bullish Phase 38 percent more of the time than did IBM, while making 294 additional 60 period channel higher highs. IBM occupied the Bearish Phase 43 percent more than did S&P 500, while making twice as many new 60 period channel lower lows.

RECAP

"There is nothing new on Wall Street or in stock speculation. What has happened in the past will happen again and again and again. This is because human nature does not change, and it's human emotion that always gets in the way of human intelligence. Of this I am sure."[1] Jesse Livermore's quote from some 75 years ago still holds the test of time. Many Wall Street pundits consider him the greatest trader who ever lived.

The phase analysis concepts, as defined, will provide both the trader and the investor with a compass for when to buy and when to sell. Phase analysis guides the individual in how capital can be deployed in the markets, showing the trader or investor the basis on which to develop a sound money management process. The relationships of phase analysis reflect the realities that human behavior repeats itself and is inherently cyclical. Consequently, phase analysis is the relationship of price behavior to the institutional "rudders," again, the distinct patterns of price behavior. Phase analysis is the ability to articulate and demonstrate the Bearish and Bullish Phases of the market as people decide when to buy or sell. The quality of price is measured as it expands or contracts through six phases of price activity. Phase analysis offers the analyst, trader, or investor the ability to objectively define price behavior into specific categories by using a combination of readily available tools. Categorizing price with specific markers allows for statistical analysis of price structure.

Additionally, the analyst or user can compare the quality of different financial instruments using these specific criteria, and can visually recognize trend behavior, enhancing objectivity and reducing subjectivity.

---

[1]Richard Smitten, *The Amazing Life of Jesse Livermore, World's Greatest Stock Trader*, Traders Press, Inc., 1999, p. 283.

Index